Best Cooking

Martha Stewart

Martha Stewart's

Quick Cook™ Menus

Martha Stewart's
Quick Cook™ Menus

Fifty-two Meals You Can Make in Under an Hour

PHOTOGRAPHS BY CHRISTOPHER BAKER

DESIGN BY LAURENCE VÉTU-KANE

CLARKSON N. POTTER, INC./PUBLISHERS
DISTRIBUTED BY CROWN PUBLISHERS, INC., NEW YORK

To Laura Herbert, Amanda O'Brien, and Kathy Powell,
for years of help, creativity, and good will,
and to Chris Baker,
for another book of the finest photography

Published by Clarkson N.
Potter, Inc., 225 Park Avenue South, New York,
New York 10003, and
represented in Canada by
the Canadian MANDA
Group.
CLARKSON N. POTTER,
POTTER, and colophon
are trademarks of Clark-
son N. Potter, Inc.

Manufactured in Japan

Library of Congress Cata-
loging-in-Publication Data
Stewart, Martha.
  Quick cook menus/by
Martha Stewart; photo-
graphs by Christopher
Baker.
  1. Quick and easy
cookery.
  2. Menus. I. Title.
TX652.S725 1988
641.5′55—dc19
88-12585 CIP
ISBN 0-517-57064-5
10 9 8 7 6
5 4 3 2 1
First Edition

Acknowledgments

The making of a book such as this is remarkably complex: the menus must be created and tested; the ingredients and methods must be accurately recorded and retested. We must choose a table setting appropriate to each meal, then it must be lit and photographed. The photographs and the text must be blended with a good design, and then comes the actual physical production of the book: the typesetting, layout, making of dummies and mechanicals, the filmstripping, platemaking, printing, proofing, and binding. And finally there is the distribution to the book-stores—no small feat in itself. Every step of this process involves a crew dedicated to a specific craft, and I want to thank all of them for helping me once again to create a beautiful book.

My sister Laura Herbert and my assistant Amanda O'Brien have worked with me for years; without their help, the preparation of the food and the styling of the tables would have been impossible.

Special thanks to Necy Fernandes for her assistance with the flowers, table settings, food, and linens; for the past six years she has been invaluable in the creation of all my books. Many thanks to Laurie Long in my office; to Dirce Martins and Renato and Renaldo for helping in the house and the garden; to Karen Marzak and Zacki Murphy for their help in the kitchen; and to Larry Kennedy, who often shopped in New York for hard-to-find ingredients—I thank him for his patience.

Helen Brandt, Melissa Neufeld, Aimee Gauthier, and Rita Christiansen lent me props from their collections of linens and tableware, and I appreciate their help.

My warmest salutations to Christopher Baker for the extraordinary photography that graces the pages of this book. He was a joy to work with, and we all admire his even temper, his speed, and his sense of beauty.

My thanks to Laurence Vétu-Kane for the lovely, fresh design that provides such a perfect setting for these photographs and for my stories.

My gratitude to all my friends at Crown and Clarkson N. Potter for their extraordinary professionalism: to Alan Mirken, the president; Bruce Harris, pub-lisher; Carol Southern, editor-in-chief; Gael Towey, creative director; Isolde Motley and Kathy Powell, my editors; Susan Magrino, my publicist; and to Amy Schuler, Laurie Stark, Jennifer Smith, and Teresa Nicholas who ensured that the book you hold in your hands is just the way I wanted it to be.

Preface

The first *Quick Cook,* published in 1983, introduced my philosophy for everyday cooking, that very excellent meals can be prepared for family and friends in an hour or less. This new *Quick Cook* volume continues that theme with lots of new recipes and even some new ways of thinking about food.

In the last five years, more of us have gone to work; with fuller lives, we have even less time to devote to cooking and housekeeping. At the same time, we have perhaps become even more conscious of what we eat—our palates are more sophisticated, and we are more aware of our health. It has been great fun addressing these concerns in this new book. I found it a challenge to invent menus that allow us to continue eating three meals a day but to consume fewer calories. There is a noticeable decrease in the use of cream and butter, more salads, less bread, and more shellfish and fish. There is certainly a greater emphasis on pasta, good soup recipes, and increased use of grains. I do more grilling over gas or wood fires and very little frying. Portions may be a bit smaller, in keeping with our desire for slimmer waistlines, but I have not sacrificed taste, presentation, or variety.

I have tried to make Quick Cooking even quicker by adding some items to our *batterie de cuisine*—a mandoline for juliennes and waffled potatoes, a compact electric slicer for apples, potatoes, other fruits and vegetables, and for meats, a food processor for soups, purees, sauces, and pastries, a pasta maker, hand grater, zester, stripper, and a really sharp cheese knife. An ice-cream maker produces sorbets and ice creams—simple and healthful desserts—in a limited time. Together with good skillets and generous pots, these tools and appliances allow us to make Quick Cooking a reality.

It was my daughter, Alexis, who really urged me to write this new book. She is now twenty-two, just the age I was when I first began cooking seriously. She is trying to find great meals to make in very limited time, and she has used the first *Quick Cook* so much that she needs new menus. She shops now just as I do, stopping at the greengrocer for vegetables and fruits, the fishmonger for the perfect fresh fish, the cheese store for the freshest small cheese, and the bakery for her favorite hard, sour baguette. This book is intended for her, and for all of us who love to feed ourselves and our families well but need new ideas, inspiration, and encouragement.

Contents

Pantry

The Quick Cook's pantry as described below may appear intimidating, but keep in mind that this is an ultimate list, including ingredients that would allow one to cook a great number of ethnic and regional dishes. Pare this list down to suit your own style of cooking—or add your own favorite ingredients.

OILS: mild olive (for frying and sautéing), extra-virgin (green) olive, safflower, oriental sesame, light vegetable, hot pepper (chile), peanut, corn, hazelnut, walnut, sunflower, avocado, grapeseed

If your family is small or if you don't cook every day, buy oils in small quantities. Keep opened cans and bottles in the refrigerator to prevent oils—especially unstable nut oils—from becoming rancid.

VINEGARS: balsamic, red wine, tarragon, Champagne, sherry, cider, Chinese black, rice wine, white distilled, blueberry, raspberry

Vinegars last much better than oils in the ordinary pantry cupboard, but it is best to keep the temperature below 65° F.

GRAINS: long-grain white rice (never instant), Arborio rice, basmati rice (white and brown), Japanese rice (Kokohu Rose), wild rice, couscous, bulgur, whole-wheat berries, quick-cooking oats, cornmeal (white and yellow), grits, unbleached white flour, whole-wheat flour, cake flour, semolina, rye flour, rice flour, cornstarch, tapioca (pearl and fine grain)

I like to transfer grains and flour from their paper wrappings into glass or plastic storage containers; flours go in wide-mouthed jars or crocks so I can dip in with a measuring spoon or cup. I refrigerate or freeze those items that I rarely use.

SUGARS: granulated, rose geranium, vanilla, dark brown, light brown, confectioners', brown rock, French coffee cubes, pralines (nut sugars), honey, molasses, corn syrup (dark and light), maple syrup

I use Mason jars with screw-on or clamp tops to store sugars.

BAKING NEEDS: baking powder, baking soda, cream of tartar, yeast (dry or fresh), shortening (Crisco), lard, vegetable oil spray, unflavored gelatin, cocoa powder, chocolate (bitter, semisweet, and white), instant espresso granules, vanilla extract, almond extract, marzipan paste

All these items should be kept well organized in the pantry or refrigerator.

NUTS AND DRIED FRUITS: pecans, hazelnuts or filberts, almonds (shelled and blanched, whole and sliced), cashews (shelled, unsalted), pignolis (pine nuts), macadamias, pistachios (shelled, unsalted), walnuts, coconut (shredded and flaked), raisins (golden, dark, and muscatel), apricots, prunes, currants, dates

I store nuts in airtight containers or plastic bags in the freezer. I always let them thaw to room temperature in the freezer wrapping before using them (never chop a frozen or cold nut—it will become very oily and damp). I store dried fruits in airtight containers in a dark, cool place.

Quick Cook Menus *includes several recipes for home-made pasta, each with a different flavor and texture.*

PASTAS: rice noodles, buckwheat noodles, Udon noodles, soba noodles, cellophane noodles, mafaldine, orzo, pastina, orecchiette, lasagna, angel hair, fettuccine, spaghetti, spaghettini, fusilli.

Dried pasta should be stored in a cool, dark place. Fresh pasta should be well wrapped in plastic and frozen immediately.

CANNED, BOTTLED, AND PACKAGED GOODS: coconut cream, barbecue sauce, anchovies, tuna, bamboo shoots, water chestnuts, dried beans (flageolets, black beans, black-eyed peas, kidney beans, navy beans, cannellini), whole chestnuts, tomato paste (cans and tubes), grape leaves, pickling lime, peach nectar, pineapple juice, cranberry juice, canned chicken and beef stock, canned pumpkin, capers (large and small), ketchup, mayonnaise, Worcestershire sauce, mustard (Dijon, coarse-grain), soy sauce, hoisin sauce, evaporated milk, condensed milk, wild blueberries in syrup, sun-dried tomatoes, whole canned tomatoes, olives (green, black), mandarin oranges, litchis, cornichons, chick-peas, jams, jellies, peanut butter

Of course, you may not need every item on this list, but one jar, can, or box of each would enable you to cook almost any dish.

FROZEN GOODS: fresh-frozen fruits (I freeze cranberries, blueberries, blackberries, raspberries, and currants on trays and then pack them in rigid containers), fruit purees and juices, pastry dough (in flat rounds and shells), cookie doughs, tortillas, breads, pesto, duck fat, bread crumbs, poppy seeds, crêpes, petit pois, homemade stocks, bacon, pancetta, margarine, lima beans, corn kernels, crumb toppings, dried mushrooms, assorted ground coffees

Remember that everything stored in the freezer must be well wrapped and labeled with a description of the item and the date it was frozen.

WINES AND SPIRITS: white wines (including sauterne), red wines, Champagne, marsala, port, sherry, cognac, armagnac, calvados, black currant liqueur (crème de cassis), raspberry liqueur (crème de framboise), orange liqueur (Grand Marnier or Cointreau), cherry liqueur (kirsch), peppermint liqueur (crème de menthe), anise liqueur (Sambuca), hazelnut liqueur (Frangelico), blackberry liqueur, vermouth, rum, gin, tequila, bourbon, Scotch, vodka, several types of beer

SPICES: peppercorns (Malabar, Tellicherry, white, green, and pink), sea salt, kosher salt, cayenne pepper, saffron, dill seed, cinnamon sticks, ground cinnamon, cumin, vanilla beans, nutmeg, ginger, allspice, mace, red pepper flakes, Cajun spice mixture, curry, turmeric, coriander, bay leaves, juniper berries, sesame seeds (black and white), whole cardamom, Old Bay seasoning, celery seed, chili powder, star anise, tandoori spice, mustard (seeds and powder), caraway seeds, pickling spice, Oriental five-spice mix, mulled cider mix, cloves (whole and ground)

PERISHABLES: Parmesan, pecorino (Locatelli), Gruyère or Emmentaler, Roquefort, cream cheese, horseradish, lemons, limes, oranges, grapefruits, scallions, milk, cream, sour cream, crème fraîche, buttermilk, unsalted butter, eggs, carrots, celery, garlic, potatoes (baking, Red Bliss, yellow), onions (white, Spanish, Vidalia, red, yellow), shallots, fresh gingerroot

HERBS: parsley, sage, basil, thyme, oregano, marjoram, tarragon, dill, coriander (cilantro), mint, bay leaves, rosemary, sorrel, savory

I rely a great deal on fresh herbs. I grow them in large, shallow flowerpots in my house during the winter and outdoors during the growing season.

The *Quick Cook* pantry does not consist solely of store-bought items. It should also include some homemade staples, like mayonnaise, pastry shells, crème fraîche, and stocks. We have provided our recipes here for your convenience.

Mayonnaise

MAKES 2½ CUPS

2 eggs
¼ teaspoon dry mustard
¾ teaspoon salt
2 tablespoons fresh lemon juice
1 cup light olive oil
1 cup vegetable or safflower oil

1. Put the eggs, mustard, salt, and lemon juice in the bowl of a food processor or a blender jar.

2. Combine the olive oil and vegetable oil. Turn on the machine and pour in the oil, drop by drop, until the mixture thickens. Add the remaining oil in a steady stream. Store, tightly covered, in refrigerator for up to 7 days.

Tart Shells

MAKES TWO 8- TO 10-INCH TARTS OR
EIGHT 4½-INCH TARTLETS

2½ cups all-purpose flour
1 teaspoon salt
1 teaspoon granulated sugar (optional)
1 cup (2 sticks) unsalted butter, chilled,
    cut into small pieces
¼ to ½ cup ice water

1. Put the flour, salt, and sugar in the bowl of a food processor. Add the butter and process for 10 seconds, or just until the mixture resembles coarse meal.

2. Add ice water, drop by drop, through the feed tube with the machine running, just until the dough holds together without being wet or sticky; do not process more than 30 seconds.

3. Turn the dough out onto a large piece of plastic wrap. Press the dough into a flat circle; wrap in the plastic and chill for at least one hour.

4. Lightly butter or spray with vegetable cooking spray the pie plate(s) or tart pan(s) you will be using. On a lightly floured board, roll out the pastry to a thickness of ⅛ inch. Place the pastry in the tart pan, pie plate, or pastry ring that has been set on a parchment-lined baking sheet and press it into the bottom edges and along the sides. Trim the pastry using scissors or a sharp paring knife or by rolling a rolling pin across the top of the pan. Unbaked pastry shells can be refrigerated, well wrapped in plastic, for up to one day; for longer storage, they can be frozen.

NOTE: To partially or completely bake unfilled pastry shells, preheat the oven to 375° F to 400° F. Carefully line the pastry with aluminum foil, pressing it into the corners and edges, and weight with beans, rice, or aluminum or ceramic weights. Bake for 15 to 18 minutes (10 to 12 minutes for a partially baked shell). When the pastry begins to color around the edges, remove the foil and weights and continue to bake just until the pastry dries out and turns a light golden color for a partially baked shell, and a deeper amber for a fully baked shell. Let cool completely on a wire rack before filling. Baked shells can be stored in tightly covered plastic containers or, well wrapped, in the freezer.

Crème Fraîche

MAKES 2 CUPS

2 cups heavy cream
2 tablespoons buttermilk or sour cream

Heat cream over low heat to 100° F. Add buttermilk and mix well. Put in covered jar and let sit at room temperature for 6 to 8 hours. Refrigerate at least 24 hours before serving. The cream will become thick like sour cream.

NOTE: Crème fraîche can be kept in the refrigerator for 2 to 3 weeks.

Chicken Stock

MAKES APPROXIMATELY 6 CUPS

1 whole (6-pound) stewing chicken
3 whole carrots, peeled
1 large yellow onion, unpeeled, halved and studded with cloves
2 white onions, unpeeled
1 red onion, peeled
2 shallots, unpeeled
3 leeks, well washed and trimmed
1 whole head of garlic, unpeeled
6 cloves garlic, peeled
3 celery stalks
3 bay leaves, preferably fresh
½ teaspoon mixed black and white whole peppercorns
Large bunch of fresh chervil or flat Italian parsley

1. Preheat the oven to 400° F.

2. Place all ingredients in a large (8-quart) Dutch oven. Add 2 cups water and roast in the oven for 30 minutes.

3. Remove the pot from the oven and add water to cover. Simmer on top of the stove for 3 to 4 hours.

4. Let the stock cool slightly, skim off any fat, and strain, reserving the chicken for another use. Refrigerate or freeze the stock in smaller amounts for future use, as needed.

NOTE: To make veal stock, add 3 to 4 pounds of veal shanks or knuckles to the chicken and vegetables in the Dutch oven and cook as directed above.

Beef Stock

MAKES APPROXIMATELY 3 CUPS

3 pounds beef shank bones, cut into 2-inch pieces
4 lean short ribs of beef
¾ pound oxtail, cut into chunks
4 leeks, well washed and split lengthwise
4 stalks celery
2 whole carrots, peeled
1 yellow onion, unpeeled, halved and studded with cloves
3 fresh bay leaves
1 large sprig of thyme
2 white spring onions, trimmed
Large bunch fresh flat Italian parsley
1 whole head of garlic, unpeeled
½ teaspoon whole black peppercorns

To make the stock, follow the method for Chicken Stock, above. (The cooked beef bones that remain after straining off the stock are delicious served simply with strong horseradish.)

Homemade chicken stock (below) and beef stock (opposite page) are easy to make, keep well in the freezer, and taste infinitely better than the canned or cubed versions.

Broiled Lamb Chops with Mint Pesto

The root vegetable soup is such a lovely color in all its variations, I like to serve it in shallow, white soup plates with just a bright green sprig of coriander for garnish.

Early spring is such a wonderful time: this is the season when I try to create fresh and exciting menus like this one, which is designed to take advantage of some of the newness of spring and, at the same time, adapt some of the old fare of winter.

The root vegetable soup has become a favorite of my family and friends and can be made with many different combinations. By adding a rutabaga, a sweet potato, or a butternut squash, the flavor can be changed dramatically. This version is mellow and mild, very pleasing to most everyone. Serve it in large, flat soup plates with an herb garnish and a sprinkling of freshly ground pepper.

When serving lamb chops, I always splurge and buy the most delectable baby loin chops I can find. Since most of us are eating less meat these days, I find that one chop per person will suffice, especially if a hearty soup is served first. Otherwise, count on two of the small chops for each person. The mint pesto is my own invention, inspired by the first fresh mint of the year: it is a simple version of the popular basil-flavored pesto we all know, with walnuts in place of pignolis, mint instead of basil, and no cheese at all. Brushed on the lamb chops while they grill, it adds a delicious and unique flavor. And don't forget to reserve a little for the parboiled onions, which grill alongside the chops.

The chops and onions complement each other so wonderfully, I added the asparagus to provide a visual and flavorful contrast. It is always fun to make something pretty for a dinner plate, and the asparagus bundles tied with little strips of leek ribbon, while very simple to produce, give the presentation a finished look.

The pineapple and orange salad is the perfect example of a Quick Cook dessert. By cutting the fruits beautifully and sprinkling them with crushed brown rock sugar, one can create a sparkling—and delicious—dessert in minutes.

M E N U

ROOT VEGETABLE SOUP
BROILED LAMB CHOPS WITH MINT PESTO
BOILED AND GRILLED ONIONS
ASPARAGUS TIED WITH LEEKS
PINEAPPLE AND ORANGE SALAD

Tying a bundle of asparagus spears with a leek "ribbon" takes only a minute, and it looks so pretty on a background of new white Wedgewood atop a white homespun table-cloth. The silver flatware is English, circa 1853, by Lias Bros.

Root Vegetable Soup

SERVES 4 TO 6

5 tablespoons unsalted butter
2 yellow onions, peeled and chopped
4 shallots, peeled and chopped
1 leek, trimmed, washed, and thinly sliced crosswise
2 cloves garlic, peeled and minced
2 parsnips, peeled and cut into ½-inch dice
2 carrots, peeled and cut into ½-inch dice
1 large celeriac (celery root), peeled and cut into ½-inch dice
3 potatoes, peeled and cut into ½-inch dice
2 white turnips, peeled and cut into ½-inch dice
1½ quarts Chicken Stock (page 13) or water
   Salt and freshly ground black pepper
   Sprigs of fresh coriander (cilantro), parsley, chervil, or watercress

1. In a large, heavy saucepan, melt the butter and slowly cook the onions, shallots, leek, and garlic until tender and soft, about 5 minutes; do not brown.

2. Add the diced root vegetables and stock. Simmer until all vegetables are soft, approximately 35 minutes. Puree in 2-cup batches in a food processor until smooth.

3. Return pureed soup to the saucepan; heat through and season to taste. Serve hot, garnished with a sprig of fresh herb.

Broiled Lamb Chops with Mint Pesto

SERVES 4

Mint Pesto
1 bunch fresh mint, leaves finely chopped
2 tablespoons very finely chopped walnuts
4 cloves garlic, peeled and minced
¼ cup olive oil

4 loin lamb chops, 1½ inches thick

1. Preheat the broiler.

2. To make the mint pesto, combine the mint, walnuts, garlic, and olive oil in a small bowl and mix well. Put aside ¼ cup pesto for onions, below.

3. Brush one side of each lamb chop with a little mint pesto. Grill under the hot broiler for 4 to 5 minutes. Turn, brush with more pesto, and grill about 4 to 5 minutes longer for medium-rare chops. Serve immediately.

Boiled and Grilled Onions

SERVES 4

1 pint baby red pearl onions
8 small white onions
¼ cup Mint Pesto (see recipe above)

1. Preheat the broiler.

2. In a large pot of boiling water, cook the pearl onions for 5 minutes; remove. Cook the white onions in the same pot for 10 minutes; remove. Drain both well and slip the skins off while still warm.

3. Toss the onions with the pesto and place in a roasting pan or baking dish. Broil 3 to 5 minutes, turning once or twice.

Asparagus Tied with Leeks

SERVES 4

1 leek, well washed
32 pencil-thin asparagus
  Salt and freshly ground black pepper

1. Cut off the root and very top of the leek leaves. Carefully remove 2 leaves, making sure they are unbruised.

2. In a large skillet, blanch the leek leaves in boiling water until tender and bright green, about 2 minutes. Remove them from the water and drain on paper towels. When the leek leaves are cool, cut each into long, ½-inch-wide strips.

3. Trim off the stalk ends of the asparagus—only the perfect green should remain, and the stalks should be the same length.

4. Blanch the asparagus in boiling water until tender but not limp, 3 to 5 minutes depending on size. Drain well.

5. Gather the asparagus into bunches of 8. Carefully tie each bunch with a strip of the leek leaf and trim the ends of the "ribbon" with kitchen scissors. Season with salt and pepper and serve.

Pineapple and Orange Salad

SERVES 4

1 ripe pineapple
2 oranges
2 cubes brown rock sugar, broken into coarse crumbs

1. Slice off the top and bottom of the pineapple with a very sharp knife and carefully cut down the sides to remove all the peel. Cut the fruit crosswise into thirds and cut sections from each approximately 1½ inches wide and ⅛ inch thick.

2. With a sharp paring knife, peel the oranges and carefully section each by cutting the fruit away from the membranes.

3. Combine the fruit sections on individual plates and sprinkle with the brown rock sugar.

I sprinkled the pineapple and orange salad with crushed brown rock sugar, which I buy in boxes from Fortnum and Mason (they call it coffee sugar) when I visit London.

Cornmeal Fried Chicken

The day we made this menu, my daughter Alexis brought her boyfriend home for the evening. I heated up the pot of white corn chowder, not telling them it was left over from a photography shoot, and served it piping hot with chopped cilantro and a dollop of crème fraîche, just as it is pictured. Sam and Alexis ate every bit; they loved the fact that the soup had texture and was spicy—Alexis said next time I make it for her I should add a whole jalapeño.

Encouraged by the success of the first course, I served them the rest of the menu. Alexis is a vegetarian, so she refused the cornmeal fried chicken, but Sam ate several pieces, as did I. The broccoli had retained its bright green color, and the browned garlic cloves were wonderful. Alexis ate almost all of them, in true vegetarian fashion. (People who eat little or no meat seem to develop a craving for spicy, highly flavored foods.)

Rhubarb is ready to pick in the garden from the middle of April until the end of May, and I always try to put plenty in the freezer for winter use. Then all through the year I can make rhubarb crisps, crumbles, pies, cakes, custards, jams, and, my favorite, rhubarb baked with vanilla sugar and a bit of heavy cream.

M E N U
WHITE CORN CHOWDER
CORNMEAL FRIED CHICKEN
BROCCOLI WITH BROWNED GARLIC
BAKED RHUBARB

White Corn Chowder

SERVES 4

3 tablespoons unsalted butter
2 cloves garlic, peeled and minced
4 shallots, peeled and chopped
½ fresh jalapeño pepper, roasted (page 24), peeled, seeded, and chopped
1 cup Chicken Stock (page 13)
3 cups white corn kernels, fresh or frozen
   Pinch of salt
1½ cups heavy cream
   Chopped fresh coriander (cilantro)
   Crème Fraîche (page 11) (optional)

1. Melt the butter in a large saucepan and sauté the garlic and shallots until tender. Stir in the jalapeño pepper and cook a minute longer.

2. Add the stock and corn to the saucepan and bring to a boil. Reduce the heat and simmer for 5 minutes.

3. Puree the mixture in a food mill and return to the saucepan. (A food mill will remove the skin from the corn kernels while retaining the soup's texture.) Season with salt and add the cream. Reheat thoroughly but do not allow the soup to come to a boil. Serve hot with a sprinkling of fresh coriander; a tablespoon of crème fraîche can be swirled into each bowl, if desired.

Cornmeal Fried Chicken

SERVES 4

1 large, bright-colored orange
1 cup milk
1 (3-pound) frying chicken, cut into
 8 pieces
⅔ cup all-purpose flour
⅔ cup yellow cornmeal
1 teaspoon salt
1 teaspoon freshly ground black pepper
4 cups sunflower oil

1. With a sharp paring knife, citrus stripper, or zester, cut several long, thin strips of orange peel. From remaining peel, grate 2 tablespoons zest. Then squeeze the juice.

2. In a large bowl, combine orange zest, 2 tablespoons orange juice, and the milk. Soak the chicken and orange-peel strips in the mixture for 30 minutes.

3. In a paper bag, combine the flour, cornmeal, salt, and pepper. Coat the chicken pieces with the flour mixture, then coat the orange-peel strips.

4. In a large skillet, heat 2 inches of oil to 350° F. Fry the chicken on all sides until golden and fully cooked, 18 to 20 minutes, then drain on paper towels. Fry the orange peel until nicely golden, several minutes, and drain on paper towels. Serve chicken hot or cold, garnished with the fried orange-peel strips.

Broccoli with Browned Garlic

SERVES 4

½ cup olive oil
12 cloves garlic, carefully peeled
1 large head broccoli, separated into
 florets
2 tablespoons (¼ stick) butter, melted

1. In a heavy skillet, heat the olive oil. Add the garlic and cook, tossing frequently to avoid burning, until all the cloves are golden brown, about 7 minutes. Remove the garlic from the oil and set aside.

2. Cook the broccoli in a large pot of boiling water just until tender, 3 to 5 minutes. Drain well and toss with the hot melted butter. Arrange on a serving platter and garnish with the browned garlic.

Baked Rhubarb

SERVES 4

8 cups fresh rhubarb, chopped in
 1-inch pieces
¾ cup vanilla sugar (see Note)
2 tablespoons (¼ stick) unsalted
 butter, cut in pieces
¼ cup heavy cream

1. Preheat the oven to 375° F.

2. Butter a large baking dish and place the rhubarb in it. Sprinkle on ½ cup of the sugar and let sit 30 minutes.

3. Pour the remaining sugar over the rhubarb and dot with butter. Bake 20 minutes.

4. Pour the cream around the rhubarb and bake 5 minutes longer.

NOTE: To make vanilla sugar, place a vanilla bean in a jar and cover with granulated sugar. Store in a tightly covered jar for at least a week.

Opposite: I have a collection of pottery plates and dishes in which I can both cook and serve baked fruits. This yellow spatterware pie plate holding the rhubarb is one of my favorites.

Grilled Red Snapper

This menu combines some of my favorite Quick Cook recipes: polenta, roasted peppers, and whole grilled fish. The red snapper can be replaced by any small, fresh whole fish—a yellowtail, a sea bass, or even a small bluefish. I find that a whole 1-pound fish is a perfect serving for one person; be sure that the fins, scales, and gills are removed before cooking, but leave the head and tail on for better visual effect.

While shopping in New York one day I found a wonderful packaged mascarpone cheese, and I created this polenta dish to make use of it. After the polenta is cooked in chicken stock, I pour it into a shallow baking dish. Cheese and pesto are placed around the perimeter, so that each cut wedge contains a bit of both.

The yellow peppers can be roasted on top of the gas flame of your stove or on the outdoor grill. I find that roasted peppers work best outdoors if one uses a covered grill and sets the flame on high. Be sure to turn the peppers frequently during roasting so the skin is evenly blackened.

For dessert, make a quick and delicious parfait of ice cream and coffee liqueur, which can be lingered over with a cup of espresso, or just by itself.

M E N U

GRILLED RED SNAPPER
POLENTA WITH MASCARPONE AND PESTO
ROASTED YELLOW PEPPERS WITH PARSLEY
SALAD OF RADICCHIO, ENDIVE, FENNEL, AND PARMESAN
ESPRESSO PARFAITS

Grilled Red Snapper

SERVES 4

4 small (1-pound) red snappers, heads and tails left on, cleaned
6 lemons
½ cup olive oil
4 teaspoons soy sauce

1. With a sharp knife, score each fish approximately ⅛ inch deep in a diagonal diamond pattern on each side. Squeeze 4 lemons, combine juice with olive oil and soy sauce; pour mixture over the fish.

2. Thinly slice the remaining 2 lemons and place the slices inside the body cavities. Let rest for 30 minutes while preparing the grill. (Remember to coat the grill grate with vegetable spray to prevent the fish from sticking and falling apart while grilling.)

3. Grill the fish over hot coals (or under a hot broiler) for 5 to 7 minutes on each side. Serve immediately.

Polenta with Mascarpone and Pesto

SERVES 4

Remember to put the mascarpone and pesto in dollops around the polenta so that when it is cut, each diner will get a little of each.

Pesto

MAKES APPROXIMATELY ¾ CUP

  2 *tablespoons pignoli (pine nuts)*
  1 *clove garlic, peeled*
  ¼ *teaspoon coarse salt*
  ⅛ *teaspoon freshly ground black pepper*
  1 *cup packed fresh basil leaves*
  ¼ *cup freshly grated Parmesan cheese*
  ¼ *cup freshly grated Romano cheese*
  ½ *cup extra-virgin (green) olive oil*

Polenta

  1 *quart Chicken Stock (page 13)*
  1 *cup polenta (coarsely ground yellow cornmeal)*
  1 *teaspoon salt*
  2 *tablespoons (¼ stick) unsalted butter*

  ¼ *to ½ cup mascarpone cheese*

1. To make the pesto, combine the pignoli, garlic, salt, pepper, basil, Parmesan, Romano, and 2 tablespoons oil in a food processor; process until finely ground. Add the remaining oil in a steady stream and process until thick and creamy. Set aside.

2. Preheat the oven to 375° F.

3. In a large saucepan, bring the chicken stock to a boil and very gradually add the cornmeal, whisking constantly with a wire whisk. Cook over low heat, stirring constantly with a wooden spoon until spoon stands up straight in the mixture, approximately 15 minutes.

4. When the polenta is done, stir in the salt and butter. Pour the polenta into a nonstick or lightly buttered baking dish, place dollops of the mascarpone cheese on top, and spoon small amounts of the pesto next to the cheese. Bake until firm, about 20 minutes.

Roasted Yellow Peppers with Parsley

SERVES 4

  4 *yellow bell peppers*
      Several sprigs flat Italian parsley, chopped

1. To roast the peppers, place the entire pepper directly on the burner of a gas stove over high heat or beneath a hot broiler. As the skin blackens, turn the pepper so that the entire surface is charred. Remove the pepper from the flame and wrap it first in a paper towel, then place it in a small plastic bag for 10 to 15 minutes to "sweat" the skin off. Then, using the paper towel the pepper is wrapped in, rub as much of the skin off the pepper as possible.

2. Quarter the peppers and remove the seeds and membranes.

3. Place the peppers on a plate and sprinkle with the chopped parsley. Serve hot or cold.

NOTE: Any variety of pepper—jalapeño, Italian frying, chile, etc.—can be roasted using this technique.

Salad of Radicchio, Endive, Fennel, and Parmesan

SERVES 4

1 head radicchio, leaves cut into 3 or 4 pieces
1 head Belgian endive, leaves cut into thirds
1 bulb fennel, stalk and core removed, leaves cut into lengthwise strips
¼ cup whole flat Italian parsley leaves

Dressing
2 tablespoons balsamic vinegar
¼ cup olive oil
1 teaspoon Dijon mustard
  Salt and freshly ground black pepper

8 ounces Parmesan cheese, sliced paper thin

Gently toss all salad greens together in a serving bowl. In a small bowl, whisk the dressing ingredients together. Toss salad with dressing, top with Parmesan strips, and serve immediately.

Espresso Parfaits

SERVES 4

1 quart rich vanilla or coffee ice cream, softened slightly
1 cup coffee-flavored liqueur (Kahlua, Tia Maria, etc.)
½ cup heavy cream
1½ teaspoons instant espresso granules
1½ teaspoons sugar

1. Alternate layers of softened ice cream and liqueur in tall parfait glasses. Set in freezer for at least 30 minutes.

2. Whip the cream, instant espresso, and sugar to soft peaks. Spoon a dollop on top of the ice cream before serving.

We served the espresso parfaits in pink Depression glass goblets, with long-handled iced tea spoons to reach down to the bottom.

Calf's Liver with Herbs

Every month or so I get a craving for a piece of calf's liver or baby beef liver. I remember my childhood doctor reminding me to eat a bit of liver for iron, and I think the craving is not only a reminder of this but also of several trips to Italy. No one serves liver in so many ways as the Italians—the most delicious, I think, are the simple sautés of liver cut in strips or squares and cooked in butter with sage leaves or, as in this recipe, with rosemary. Peas with pancetta is an adaptation of another Italian recipe combining fresh young vegetables with that wonderful cured Italian bacon and fresh herbs.

Japanese honey mushrooms look like brown enoki mushrooms and have a bit more flavor than their white counterparts. Of course, one can substitute dried porcini (remember they must be soaked before cooking) or Polish wood mushrooms. Even white button mushrooms—which assume a much better flavor if thinly sliced and cooked in butter until dark golden brown—can be used. Combined with mushrooms, sautéed cabbage is quick, easy, and ultimately delicious.

To end the meal, try this very simple lime sorbet atop a ripe papaya slice. The limes are prepared with a zester, a handy tool with five small, sharp holes, which removes the brightly colored skin of the fruit in long, thin threads.

For one of my favorite dishes— calf's liver with herbs—I chose my favorite contemporary plates, classic-style drabware from Wedgewood. The teal blue glass goblets are early twentieth-century Tiffany, and the plaid napkins are from the Ralph Lauren collection.

M E N U

CALF'S LIVER WITH HERBS
PEAS AND PANCETTA
CABBAGE WITH MUSHROOMS
LIME SORBET

Calf's Liver with Herbs

SERVES 2

½ pound calf's liver, sliced ¼ inch thick
¼ cup all-purpose flour
½ teaspoon coarsely chopped fresh
  rosemary leaves
3 tablespoons unsalted butter
2 cloves garlic, peeled and thinly sliced
2 large sprigs fresh rosemary
2 large lemon wedges
  Salt and freshly ground black pepper

1. Cut the liver into 1-inch squares and dredge very lightly in the flour. Sprinkle the crushed rosemary over the liver and set aside.

2. In a small skillet, melt the butter and sauté the garlic just until golden, 2 to 3 minutes. Remove the garlic and continue to heat the butter until it begins to foam. Add the liver, rosemary leaves, and rosemary sprigs, and sauté the liver 1 to 2 minutes on each side. Do not overcook. Season and serve hot with the sautéed rosemary sprigs and the lemon wedges.

Opposite: *With a little thought, fresh fruits and vegetables can become wonderful "serving dishes" for soups, sauces, and, especially, sorbets. See how this homemade lime sorbet sits on a "plate" of fresh papaya.*

Peas and Pancetta

SERVES 2

1 tablespoon unsalted butter
  Pinch of sugar
1 cup fresh or frozen baby peas
1 tablespoon olive oil
½ cup finely diced pancetta (Italian
  unsmoked bacon)
½ teaspoon torn fresh sage leaves

1. Place the butter and sugar in a small saucepan of boiling water. Add the peas and blanch just until tender, 1 to 2 minutes. Drain well.

2. In a small skillet, heat the olive oil and sauté the pancetta. As soon as the fat is rendered, add the peas and sage leaves. Toss gently to warm; serve.

Cabbage with Mushrooms

SERVES 2

2 ounces Japanese honey mushrooms
½ tablespoon unsalted butter
1 clove garlic, peeled and finely minced
1 shallot, peeled and finely minced
3 tablespoons olive oil
½ small head green cabbage, finely
  shredded
  Salt and freshly ground black pepper
5 or 6 fresh mint leaves

1. In a small skillet, sauté the mushrooms in the butter for 1 to 2 minutes.

2. In a medium skillet, sauté the garlic and shallot in the oil until tender but not brown, about 5 minutes. Add the cabbage and cook just until wilted, approximately 4 to 5 minutes. Add the mushrooms to the cabbage, season to taste, and stir in the mint leaves. Serve immediately.

Lime Sorbet

MAKES 1½ PINTS

½ cup sugar
2 cups water
½ cup fresh lime juice
  Zest of ½ lime

1 ripe papaya

1. Place the sugar and 1 cup of water in a heavy, noncorroding saucepan. Cook over medium heat until the sugar is completely dissolved. Remove from the heat and stir in the remaining water, lime juice, and most of the zest (reserve some for garnish). Chill thoroughly.

2. Freeze the mixture in an ice-cream maker according to the manufacturer's directions.

3. Serve on a seeded slice of ripe papaya, garnished with remaining lime zest.

Pan-cooked Trout with Tomatoes and Herbs

M y childhood memories of early spring always seem to involve my older brother Eric. It was he who taught me to shoot, to trap, to tie flies, and to fish. On the opening day of trout season, he would take me on an early-morning bicycle ride to a rushing stream, where we would stake our claim to the most opportune spot before anyone else arrived. In those days it was my job to gut and clean the catch, and my mother's job to cook it: she would dust the fish with seasoned flour and toss it into a black iron skillet in which a bit of butter had melted. Although I do not now hunt to kill, I do still fish—and there are few things I like better than freshly caught trout simply cooked in a pan.

In this menu the trout is sautéed with fresh basil, olive oil, a bit of garlic, and some fresh tomatoes. When I cook whole fish these days, I usually fill the cavity with a handful of fresh herbs; this simple addition gives the trout such good flavor I serve it with only plain boiled potatoes, fresh green beans, and fava beans.

Good grapefruits are still available in spring. For this dessert try to mix white grapefruit with Marsh Ruby reds, and take care to cut them nicely. Cutting perfect grapefruit sections is not difficult, but it requires good tools and practice. First cut away the top and bottom of the skin so the fruit can sit flat on a cutting board. With a very sharp knife, cut off the entire skin and white pith, down to the flesh. Then, holding the fruit in the palm of your hand, cut away each section as close to the membrane as possible. When all the sections have been removed, squeeze all the juice from the membranes over the fruit to keep it moist until serving time, when you arrange the sections prettily on individual plates and flavor them with a sprinkling of Cointreau.

I am always happy when a cookpot can double as a serving dish: the old copper oval pan in which these trout were sautéed and brought to table, for example, is a great favorite. The rest of this table setting is a nice mélange of my favorite greens —wooden-handled flatware, an old set of nesting bowls, Italian dinner plates, and an old pair of square green-glass salt and pepper cellars.

M E N U

BOILED POTATOES WITH GREEN OLIVE OIL
PAN-COOKED TROUT WITH TOMATOES AND HERBS
TWO-BEAN SAUTÉ
RED AND WHITE GRAPEFRUIT SECTIONS WITH COINTREAU

Boiled Potatoes with Green Olive Oil

SERVES 2

3 red-skinned new potatoes, 1 to 1½ inches in diameter
3 white-skinned new potatoes, 1 to 1½ inches in diameter
2 tablespoons green olive oil
   Salt and freshly ground black pepper

1. With a sharp vegetable peeler, remove a strip of skin ¼ to ⅓ inch wide from the center of each potato.

2. In a pot of simmering (not boiling) water, cook the potatoes until just tender, about 10 minutes. Drain well.

3. Place the potatoes in a serving bowl and drizzle with olive oil to taste. Sprinkle with salt and pepper and serve.

Pan-cooked Trout with Tomatoes and Herbs

SERVES 2

2 tablespoons olive oil
2 cloves garlic, peeled and sliced
2 (1-pound) brook or rainbow trout, cleaned, with heads and tails left on
   Sprigs of fresh basil, parsley, and chervil
6 plum tomatoes, peeled, seeded, and chopped
2 tablespoons torn fresh basil leaves

1. In a large skillet, heat the olive oil over high heat. Add the garlic slices and sauté just until golden brown, about 5 minutes. Set garlic aside.

2. Dry the trout with paper towels and stuff the cavities with the fresh herb sprigs. Tie the trout closed with a bit of kitchen string or butcher's twine.

3. Sauté the fish in the hot olive oil for 4 minutes on each side. Reduce the heat and add the chopped tomatoes, basil leaves, and reserved garlic. Cover and simmer for 8 to 10 minutes. Serve immediately.

Two-Bean Sauté

SERVES 2

½ pound fresh green beans
½ pound shelled fresh fava beans
2 tablespoons green olive oil
1 tablespoon unsalted butter
   Salt and freshly ground black pepper

1. In separate pots of boiling water, blanch each type of bean until just tender and bright green, 3 to 4 minutes. Drain.

2. Combine the olive oil and butter in a medium skillet. Add the beans and quickly sauté for 3 or 4 minutes. Season with salt and pepper and serve.

Red and White Grapefruit Sections with Cointreau

SERVES 2

1 small red grapefruit
1 small white grapefruit
1 tablespoon Cointreau

1. With a very sharp knife, remove the rind and white pith from the grapefruits. Section the fruits carefully, cutting between the membranes so the sections come out whole.

2. Arrange the grapefruit in a decorative pattern on individual dessert plates. Pour a bit of Cointreau over each and chill until ready to serve.

Crab Fritters

I think this whole menu was an excuse to serve orange bourbon sours from my sister Laura's cobalt blue martini shaker; somehow the sours inspired a meal of casual Southern flavors.

Many people have their own special recipe for crab cakes or fritters, and this is just our version. Note that it doesn't have mayonnaise in it and that it is made with fresh lump crabmeat. I get my crabmeat from Balducci's in New York, which is supplied by Obrycki's, the famous Baltimore crab house.

One can pick up new ideas for serving food just about anywhere: I was watching late-night television when I saw the chef from Le Cirque make fried potato nests for sautéed quail. He made the nests from waffle-cut potato slices—a mandoline is necessary for cutting potatoes this way, but it's worth the investment. The waffles are very pretty and fry up quickly to a golden brown—they are especially good if cooked in olive oil, as they were here.

Tomatillos are little green tomatoes often used in Mexican cooking; they have a taste all their own. The cabbage slaw can be made from green, red, or Chinese cabbage, and it is dressed up with strips of julienned red and yellow peppers and flavored with fresh dill and dill seed.

This blueberry crisp is always a huge success whether it's served alone or with a scoop of vanilla ice cream. If you can find small, wild blueberries or cultivated Maine blueberries, this dessert will be even more delicious.

We made orange bourbon sours in honor of Laura's cobalt-blue Depression glass cocktail shaker, and the rest of this crab fritter dinner just evolved from there. Even the salt and pepper shakers and the stick stirrers are Depression glass. The flatware is my Gorham sterling, a wedding present from my in-laws.

M E N U

ORANGE BOURBON SOURS
CRAB FRITTERS
CABBAGE SLAW
WAFFLE FRIES
SAUTÉED TOMATILLOS
BLUEBERRY CRISP

Orange Bourbon Sours

SERVES 4

2 cups orange juice (preferably fresh)
½ cup fresh lemon juice
¼ cup sugar
½ cup good bourbon
Chipped ice
Thick orange slices, for garnish

1. Combine juices, sugar, and bourbon and stir or shake until the sugar is completely dissolved.

2. Pour the drink over chipped ice and garnish with orange slices.

NOTE: This drink can also be made in a blender with a couple of ice cubes.

Crab Fritters

SERVES 4

1 shallot, peeled and finely minced
8 tablespoons (1 stick) unsalted butter
1 tablespoon all-purpose flour
2 eggs, lightly beaten
1 pound lump crabmeat, picked over, with shell and cartilage removed
3 scallions, thinly sliced
1 cup fresh bread crumbs
1 tablespoon chopped fresh parsley
1 tablespoon chopped fresh dill
   Salt and freshly ground black pepper
3 limes, cut into 4 wedges each

1. Sauté the shallot in 1 tablespoon of butter.

2. In a large bowl, gently mix all ingredients except remaining butter and the limes. Do not overstir or the crabmeat will break into small pieces.

3. In a large frying pan, heat the remaining butter until foamy.

4. Form the crabmeat mixture into small, thick pancakes and fry until golden brown, 3 to 4 minutes on each side, adding butter to the pan as necessary. Serve immediately with the lime wedges.

Cabbage Slaw

SERVES 4

½ head green cabbage, shredded
1 red bell pepper, seeded, cored, and julienned
1 yellow bell pepper, seeded, cored, and julienned
2 tablespoons chopped fresh dill
1 tablespoon dill seed
½ cup Mayonnaise (page 11)
   Salt and freshly ground black pepper

Combine all ingredients except the salt and pepper in a large bowl and toss until well mixed. Season to taste. Chill until ready to serve.

Waffle Fries

SERVES 4

3 large baking potatoes, peeled
2 cups olive oil
   Salt to taste

1. Using a mandoline slicer, cut the potatoes with the waffle blade, turning the potatoes 90 degrees after making each slice. (This will give you a waffle effect on both sides.) Set aside.

2. Heat the olive oil in a skillet over medium-high heat. Cook the potatoes a small batch at a time until golden brown, approximately 6 to 9 minutes. Drain well on paper towels.

3. Sprinkle the potatoes with salt and serve hot.

Sautéed Tomatillos

SERVES 4

5 small tomatillos (Mexican green tomatoes)
1 tablespoon olive oil
1 tablespoon unsalted butter

1. Remove the paper husks from the tomatillos and cut them into ¼-inch-thick slices.

2. In a small skillet, heat the olive oil and butter over medium heat. Add the tomatillos and sauté on both sides until tender and golden, 6 to 8 minutes.

I baked this blueberry crisp in a rectangular Pillivuyt ovenproof dish and served it warm with scoops of vanilla ice cream, the perfect end to an all-American feast.

Blueberry Crisp

SERVES 4

¾ cup all-purpose flour
½ cup sugar
½ teaspoon ground cinnamon
6 tablespoons (¾ stick) unsalted butter, chilled
5 cups blueberries, fresh or frozen
Vanilla ice cream (optional)

1. Preheat the oven to 375° F.

2. Combine the flour, sugar, and cinnamon in a bowl; blend in the butter with a pastry cutter or your fingers until the mixture is crumbly.

3. Place the blueberries in a buttered baking dish and sprinkle the crumb mixture over them. Bake about 20 minutes. Serve warm with vanilla ice cream, if desired.

Veal Scallopini with Sage

Every Quick Cook should have a repertoire of veal recipes; this tender meat responds well to speedy, simple preparation. It is very important, however, to get the right kind and cut of veal. Meat from the leg is traditionally used for scallopini—it is very finely textured. For this recipe particularly, the veal should be cut very thin so it needs no pounding. (When scallops are quickly sautéed, I find that pounded veal shrinks and toughens.)

This veal dish could not be simpler. You might recognize it as a variation of veal piccata—scallopini flavored with lemon—but we saved the lemon flavor for the pasta in this menu. We used a dry pasta called *mafaldine,* from the Abruzzi region of Italy: about half an inch thick, with ruffled edges, *mafaldine* is designed to hold a sauce. The baby eggplant and squash atop a mound of fresh ricotta cheese is a dish I have been making for my family for years.

When I serve a main-course pasta dish, I often end the meal with a light, fruit-based dessert. This sorbet of fresh or frozen blackberries is a perfect example: it has a lovely, clean, cool taste and it is especially pretty with a few lush berries scattered on the side.

M E N U

VEAL SCALLOPINI WITH SAGE
PASTA WITH TOMATO-LEMON SAUCE
BABY VEGETABLES WITH RICOTTA CHEESE
RED OAKLEAF SALAD WITH CAPERS
BLACKBERRY SORBET WITH FRESH BLACKBERRIES

Veal Scallopini with Sage

SERVES 4

2 tablespoons (¼ stick) unsalted butter
3 cloves garlic, peeled
1 to 1¼ pounds veal scallops, cut very
   thinly from the leg
   All-purpose flour for dusting
16 fresh sage leaves

1. Melt the butter in a large skillet and add the whole cloves of garlic. Sauté for 3 to 5 minutes; do not brown the butter or garlic.

2. Lightly dust the veal scallops with a bit of flour and put them in the hot skillet; tuck sage leaves under the scallops so that they stick to the meat. Sauté for 2 minutes and turn over, then sauté just 2 minutes longer. Serve immediately.

Pasta with Tomato–Lemon Sauce

SERVES 4

1 tablespoon unsalted butter
2 tablespoons finely chopped shallots
6 sun-dried tomatoes, cut lengthwise
   into thin strips
1 cup heavy cream
1 sprig fresh oregano, plus leaves for
   garnish
   Large pinch of saffron threads
8 ounces mafaldine, or another long,
   curly pasta
   Salt and freshly ground white pepper
   Zest of 1 lemon

1. In a large skillet, melt the butter and quickly sauté the shallots, 2 to 3 min-

utes. Add the tomatoes, cream, oregano, and saffron. Simmer until the sauce is reduced by one-third.

2. While the sauce is simmering, cook the pasta in a large pot of boiling water until tender, 8 to 10 minutes. Drain well and keep warm.

3. When the sauce is reduced, add the salt and white pepper to taste and sprinkle on the lemon zest. Serve immediately over the hot pasta and garnish with fresh oregano leaves.

Baby Vegetables with Ricotta Cheese

SERVES 4

8 to 12 tiny Japanese eggplants, 1 to 2
   inches long
16 to 20 assorted tiny squash (we used
   courgettes—baby zucchini—and
   pattypan squash)
1 tablespoon olive oil
   Salt and freshly ground black pepper
½ cup whole-milk ricotta cheese

1. In a large pot of boiling water, blanch the eggplants until tender, 6 to 8 minutes. Drain.

2. In a separate pot of boiling water, blanch the squash until tender, 4 to 6 minutes. Drain.

3. Heat the olive oil in a large skillet and quickly add the blanched baby vegetables. Sauté until hot, 3 to 4 minutes, then season to taste.

4. To serve, put 2 tablespoons ricotta on each plate and top with a portion of the vegetables.

Red Oakleaf Salad with Capers

SERVES 4

1 handful per person of baby red oakleaf lettuce

Dressing
MAKES ½ CUP

2 tablespoons balsamic vinegar
¼ cup olive oil
1 teaspoon Dijon mustard
  Salt and freshly ground black pepper

2 tablespoons imported capers, drained

Place the lettuce in a large bowl. Whisk together all ingredients for the dressing and toss with the lettuce. Sprinkle the capers on top of the salad and serve.

Blackberry Sorbet with Fresh Blackberries

MAKES 1 PINT

3½ to 4 cups blackberries, fresh or frozen
⅔ cup water
6 tablespoons sugar
2 tablespoons blackberry liqueur

1. In a medium saucepan, combine 3 cups of blackberries, water, and sugar and bring to a boil. Reduce heat and let mixture simmer for 2 to 3 minutes; sugar must be completely dissolved.

2. Put the blackberry mixture through a fine sieve, pushing with a wooden spoon to strain out the seeds. Stir in the blackberry liqueur and chill thoroughly.

3. Put the blackberry mixture in an ice-cream maker and freeze according to the manufacturer's directions.

4. Serve the blackberry sorbet with the remaining whole blackberries.

This purple blackberry sorbet provides another example of how a wonderfully colored dessert should be served on the simplest dish.

Pan-fried Shad Roe

The season for shad and shad roe is very short—just about three weeks in Connecticut, where we live—and I always try to eat the roe three or four times before it disappears for another year. Sometimes I parboil the roe, peel it, flour it, and sauté it, but for this menu I simply fried the roe in lots of butter, seasoning it lightly with salt and pepper.

Baby artichokes sometimes appear for short periods at the same time as shad roe, and they are a wonderful side dish. Very tiny, tender artichokes can just be boiled and quartered; if they are large and tough, they must be trimmed of their prickly leaves, boiled for about 20 minutes, then quartered and cored. Sautéed with boiled new potatoes in olive oil flavored with fresh marjoram and a bit of butter, they are excellent.

Poached pears are usually prepared in a light sugar syrup or in sweetened, flavored wine, but for this recipe we poached them in rosehip tea, which imparts a unique and lovely taste to the fruit. Served with a hot fudge sauce (this can be made in advance), the pears are an elegant yet easy dessert. Remember to cut a bit off the bottom of each pear so they will stand upright on the dessert plates.

I always associate shad roe with spring planting—hence the seed packets. The wine goblet is Sandwich glass, and the knife and fork came from New York's old Commodore Hotel. (It is often possible to buy wonderful china and flatware from hotels that are changing hands or being demolished.)

M E N U

PAN-FRIED SHAD ROE
ARTICHOKE-POTATO SAUTÉ
RED LEAF-LETTUCE SALAD
ROSEHIP PEARS WITH HOT FUDGE SAUCE

Pan-fried Shad Roe

SERVES 2

2 small pairs fresh shad roe (see Note)
  Salt and freshly ground black pepper
4 to 6 tablespoons unsalted butter
  Lemon wedges
  Fresh parsley

1. Season the shad roe with salt and pepper. Melt the butter in a large skillet. Add the shad roe and sauté, turning carefully once (and adding more butter if necessary), until just barely tender to the touch, approximately 8 minutes. Do not overcook.

2. Remove the shad roe from the skillet and, with the point of a sharp knife, remove any visible veins or loose membrane from the inner edges.

3. Separate the pairs of shad roe and serve immediately with fresh lemon wedges and fresh parsley.

NOTE: Each serving of roe should be approximately ½ pound. One small pair per person is preferable, but you can also split a 1-pound pair between two people.

Artichoke-Potato Sauté

SERVES 2

6 miniature globe artichokes
6 small red-skinned potatoes,
  preferably Red Bliss
3 tablespoons olive oil
1 tablespoon unsalted butter
¼ cup chopped fresh marjoram
  Salt and freshly ground black pepper

1. Trim the artichokes and cook them in a large pot of boiling water until tender, approximately 15 minutes. Drain well, and when cool enough to handle, cut them into quarters.

2. Boil the potatoes until just tender, about 10 minutes. Drain, let cool slightly, and quarter them.

3. Combine the olive oil and butter in a large skillet, and when hot, add the vegetables, marjoram, and salt and pepper to taste. Sauté until brown and crispy, approximately 7 minutes. Serve immediately.

Red Leaf-Lettuce Salad

SERVES 2

1 handful of red leaf lettuce,
  preferably Salad Bowl, per person

Dressing
MAKES ¼ CUP
1 tablespoon fresh lemon juice
3 tablespoons olive oil
  Salt and freshly ground black pepper

Put the washed and dried salad greens in a serving bowl. Combine lemon juice and oil, season to taste, and toss with the lettuce right before serving.

Rosehip Pears with Hot Fudge Sauce

SERVES 2

2 ripe, firm pears, preferably Comice
  or Bartlett
4 rosehip tea bags

Hot Fudge Sauce
MAKES APPROXIMATELY 1½ CUPS
¼ cup unsweetened cocoa powder
½ cup sugar
½ cup light corn syrup
¼ cup light cream or evaporated milk
⅛ teaspoon salt
1½ tablespoons unsalted butter
½ teaspoon vanilla extract

1. Carefully peel the pears, leaving the stems intact. Cut a little slice off the bottom so they will stand upright. Place them in a deep saucepan with water to cover. Bring the water to a boil, add the tea bags, and reduce the heat to a simmer. Poach the pears until tender, 25 to 35 minutes. Let cool in the liquid.

2. To make the sauce, combine all ingredients except the vanilla in a saucepan and cook over medium heat, stirring constantly, until the mixture comes to a full boil. Boil the mixture briskly for 3 minutes, stirring occasionally, then remove from the heat and stir in the vanilla.

3. To serve, spoon pools of warm sauce onto individual dessert plates and stand pears on top; spoon more sauce over the pears.

NOTE: The hot fudge sauce can be stored in the refrigerator for 1 week. To reheat, place the container of sauce in a pan of hot—not boiling—water until the sauce warms and thins to a pouring consistency.

When choosing the service for a dish, always consider your guests' comfort: this glistening chocolate-glazed pear is served on a full-size dinner plate with a knife and fork for easier handling.

Smoked Chicken and Noodle Salad

I am very fond of old-fashioned portion plates; they remind me of college days— though at college we were never served anything as exotic as the smoked chicken and noodle salad shown here on Universal Cambridge plates. The blue and white herringbone teacups are Japanese Imari, and the cabbage platter is English, made by Adams in the late nineteenth century when Japonisme was the height of fashion.

I have always loved Oriental food, but for a long time I did not cook it at home —I thought its preparation was mysterious and preferred to leave the cooking to restaurant chefs and friends who had studied Asian cuisine for years. My daughter, Alexis, had no such hesitation; she has read a good deal about Chinese and Japanese cooking and often prepares spicy noodles, cabbage dishes, and other delicacies for us.

Alexis has taught me one secret to Oriental cooking: you must have the right ingredients. I make it a point to buy the spices and sauces in small quantities, and I keep all opened jars and bottles in a special section in my refrigerator so I know exactly where they are. I also keep a good stock of various Oriental noodles on hand in the pantry.

The smoked chicken for the main course can be made at home—a recipe for sugar-tea smoked chicken is in my book *Hors d'Oeuvres*. Smoked chickens can also be bought in many gourmet grocery stores.

The recipe for the sautéed string beans is from Amanda O'Brien, one of my assistants. The spicy sweet-and-sour cabbage tastes very good right after it is made —but even better if made a day ahead. Note that this recipe calls for a long list of ingredients; omitting one or more really does do harm to the final outcome. The thin slices of daikon, for example, add crunchiness, and the coriander leaves add a wonderful element of flavor.

The tangerine sorbet is extraordinarily good. Try to find large, juicy, flavorful tangerines or use mandarins or clementines. I make a habit of buying lots of these fruits when they are in season and then freezing the juice in one-pint plastic containers. With the containers well marked and easy to find in the freezer, wonderful sorbets can be made at any time of the year.

M E N U

SMOKED CHICKEN AND NOODLE SALAD
SPICY SWEET-AND-SOUR CABBAGE
SAUTÉED STRING BEANS
TANGERINE SORBET

Smoked Chicken and Noodle Salad

Dressing
- ¼ cup oriental sesame oil
- ¼ cup soy sauce
- 1½ tablespoons Chinese black vinegar
- 1½ tablespoons sugar
- 1 teaspoon salt
- 1 tablespoon hot pepper oil
- ¼ cup thinly sliced scallions (white and green parts)

- 1 pound Japanese whole-wheat pasta (soba)
- 2 small Japanese eggplants, unpeeled and very finely julienned
- 1 yellow bell pepper, halved, seeded, and cut into 1-inch triangular pieces
- 1 clove garlic, peeled and thinly sliced lengthwise
- 1 teaspoon peanut oil
- 1 (3-pound) smoked chicken

1. Combine all dressing ingredients, whisking well.

2. Cook the pasta in a large pot of boiling water until tender, 8 to 10 minutes. Drain well and toss in a large bowl with the dressing. Set aside.

3. Sauté the eggplants, pepper, and garlic in the peanut oil over low heat until the pepper is soft but not limp. Add the vegetables to the noodles and stir.

4. Carefully remove the wings and legs from the chicken. Thinly slice the breast meat, leaving a bit of browned skin wherever possible.

5. Place the wings, legs, and slices of smoked chicken on a large platter and spoon the noodles and vegetables alongside. Serve at room temperature.

Spicy Sweet-and-Sour Cabbage

- 1½ to 2 pounds bok choy (Chinese cabbage)
- 1½ teaspoons coarse salt
- ½ red bell pepper
- 1 small daikon (Japanese white radish)
- 16 fresh coriander (cilantro) leaves

Dressing
- 1 tablespoon dry sherry
- 1 tablespoon white wine vinegar
- ½ tablespoon rice wine vinegar
- 1 tablespoon oriental sesame oil
- 2 tablespoons sugar
- 3 cloves garlic, peeled and finely minced
- 1 teaspoon finely chopped fresh ginger
- 2 tablespoons soy sauce
- 1 teaspoon hot pepper oil
- 1 teaspoon hoisin sauce

1. Separate the leaves from the bok choy. Keep the small, inner white leaves whole; cut the large, outer green leaves into triangles of approximately the same size. Place the cabbage in a large bowl and sprinkle the salt over it (this will wilt the cabbage). Set aside.

2. Remove the seeds and membranes from the pepper and chop it into small pieces. Trim a 3-inch piece from the daikon and thinly slice it on the diagonal. Place the pepper, daikon, and coriander in a large bowl.

3. Drain the cabbage well and place it in the bowl with the other vegetables.

4. Combine dressing ingredients in a small mixing bowl and whisk well. Pour over the vegetables and toss.

Sautéed String Beans

SERVES 4

1 pound fresh string beans, stems removed
3 cloves garlic, peeled and thinly sliced
3 tablespoons olive oil
½ cup Chicken Stock (page 13)
⅛ teaspoon red pepper flakes
¼ teaspoon sugar
1 teaspoon hot pepper oil
1 tablespoon soy sauce
1 tablespoon oriental sesame oil
2 tablespoons finely chopped scallions
1½ teaspoons cornstarch
1 tablespoon water

1. In a large pot of boiling water, blanch the string beans until bright green, 2 to 3 minutes. Drain well.

2. In a wok or heavy skillet, sauté the string beans and garlic in the olive oil for 2 minutes. Add the remaining ingredients, except for the cornstarch and water, and cook 4 minutes longer.

3. Mix the cornstarch with the water until smooth. Add to the string beans, tossing to thicken the sauce, and serve immediately.

Tangerine Sorbet

MAKES 1 PINT

2 tablespoons sugar
2 cups fresh tangerine juice
1 tablespoon grated tangerine zest

1. In a heavy saucepan, combine the sugar with ½ cup of the juice. Cook over low heat until the sugar dissolves.

2. Remove the mixture from the heat and stir in the remaining tangerine juice and the zest. Chill thoroughly.

3. Freeze the tangerine mixture in an ice-cream maker according to the manufacturer's directions. Serve with mandarin orange sections and fortune cookies.

Whenever I travel, I try to find fabric that expresses the character of the country I'm in. I bought the silk for these napkins, for example, on a trip to China. The W. S. George green crackled bowls, however, are plain American—a friend found them in a country cabin and sent them to me just because they're my favorite color.

Oven-baked Halibut with Herb Butter

P art of being a good Quick Cook is having the ability to plan ahead, cook ahead, and preserve some favorite foods for future consumption. I have found few main courses that don't lose most of their character in the freezer —pastas and sauces, if frozen separately, are an exception. But breads, pastry, some cakes and cookies, and soups freeze very well: this yellow pepper soup, for example, can be made ahead, frozen, and reheated without loss of flavor.

The baked halibut represents quite another aspect of quick cooking. It is rewarding to find an impeccably fresh fish and to cook it speedily and simply—our halibut needed only a bit of herb butter to enhance its already wonderful flavor.

Cooked cucumbers are like a whole new vegetable for those who have never tasted them, and they are worth trying. The salad of limestone lettuce with beet dressing reminds me of my daughter, who always begged me to buy the tight, crispy little heads, which were packed in wooden mushroom boxes at the greengrocer and were especially dirty with rich, black soil. Limestone lettuces are a type of winter lettuce grown in greenhouses. They have very crunchy leaves, green at the edges with white hearts, and look very pretty halved or quartered and arranged on salad plates; if you can't find them, though, you can substitute small heads of Bibb or Boston lettuce.

At the end of each summer I make gallons of syrup from our quinces and freeze it in quart containers to use for ice cream, jellies, glazes, and flavoring. If you don't put up your own quinces, store-bought quince jelly can be substituted.

The pepper soup is such a strong, clear yellow, it's especially important to find the right color scheme for the table. This blue and white pattern china from Terschen-Reuth in Bavaria is perfect—the soup, with its finishing dollop of crème fraîche, seems to glow in contrast.

M E N U

YELLOW PEPPER SOUP
HERB TOASTS
OVEN-BAKED HALIBUT WITH HERB BUTTER
SAUTÉED CUCUMBERS
LIMESTONE LETTUCE WITH BEET DRESSING
QUINCE ICE CREAM

Here, the delicate blues and whites of the china and the organdy Madeira tablecloth do not overwhelm the baked halibut and cucumbers; bits of stronger color are provided by the beet dressing and by the flowers.

Yellow Pepper Soup

SERVES 4 TO 6

1 tablespoon olive oil
4 tablespoons (½ stick) unsalted butter
6 yellow bell peppers, halved, seeded, and thinly sliced
3 shallots, peeled and thinly sliced
1 clove garlic, peeled and thinly sliced
1 pear, peeled, quartered, and thinly sliced
1 quart Chicken Stock (page 13)
2 roasted yellow bell peppers (page 24), peeled, halved, seeded, and thinly sliced
   Dash of cayenne pepper
   Salt and freshly ground white pepper
¼ cup heavy cream
   Crème Fraîche (page 11)
   Herb Toasts (recipe follows)

1. Heat the oil and butter in a large saucepan and sauté the sliced vegetables and pear over medium heat until tender, 5 to 10 minutes.

2. Add the stock, roasted peppers, cayenne, and salt and pepper to taste. Bring to a boil and simmer, covered, for 30 minutes.

3. Puree the soup in small batches (approximately 2 cups each) in a food processor or blender. Pour the soup into the pan, add the heavy cream, and reheat over low heat.

4. Serve the soup hot, with a dollop of crème fraîche and the herb toasts.

Herb Toasts

SERVES 4 TO 6

Herb Butter
MAKES ¾ CUP
½ cup (1 stick) unsalted butter, at room temperature

2 tablespoons chopped fresh dill
2 tablespoons chopped fresh chervil
   Salt and freshly ground black pepper

1 loaf French bread

1. To make the herb butter, combine the butter and herbs in a small bowl and blend thoroughly. Season to taste. Keep refrigerated until ready to use.

2. Cut the French bread diagonally into ½-inch slices. Spread each with a bit of the herb butter and toast under the broiler or in the oven until crisp and browned.

NOTE: If you won't be using the herb butter within 1 day (or if you have leftovers), it should be frozen.

Oven-baked Halibut with Herb Butter

SERVES 4

2 small (1-pound) halibut steaks, 1 to 1½ inches thick
   Herb Butter (see recipe above)

1. Preheat the oven to 425° F. Butter a large baking dish.

2. Place the halibut steaks in the buttered dish; if the steaks are too large, divide them in two by cutting around the bone with a sharp knife. Dot with some of the herb butter. Cover the fish with a piece of parchment paper.

3. Bake the halibut for 5 minutes. Remove the parchment paper, dot with more herb butter, and bake approximately 5 minutes longer; the meat should be white at the bone. Serve hot.

Sautéed Cucumbers

SERVES 4

2   cucumbers
2   tablespoons (¼ stick) unsalted butter
    Salt and freshly ground white pepper
1   tablespoon fresh chervil leaves

1. Peel the cucumbers and halve them lengthwise. Using a spoon, scoop out the seeds. Cut the cucumbers into ¼-inch-thick slices.

2. Melt the butter in a medium skillet and sauté the cucumbers until softened, approximately 3 minutes. Season, garnish with the chervil, and serve.

Limestone Lettuce with Beet Dressing

SERVES 4

4   small heads limestone lettuce
2   baked beets (page 216), peeled
2   eggs
2   tablespoons fresh lemon juice
½   cups safflower oil
    Salt to taste

1. Halve the heads of lettuce and place 2 halves on each salad plate. Refrigerate.

2. Finely chop 1 beet and julienne the other into matchstick-size pieces.

3. To make the dressing, combine the eggs and lemon juice in a blender or food processor. With the motor running, slowly add just enough oil to reach a thin mayonnaise consistency. Season with salt. Add the chopped beet to the mixture and puree until smooth. Refrigerate.

4. To serve, spoon a small amount of the dressing over the lettuce and garnish with the julienned beet.

Quince Ice Cream

MAKES APPROXIMATELY 1 PINT

8   ounces quince jelly
½   cup half-and-half
3   egg yolks
1¼ cups heavy cream
¼   teaspoon vanilla extract

1. In a small saucepan, melt the quince jelly and mix with the half-and-half.

2. Beat the egg yolks lightly and add them to the quince mixture. Turn the heat to low and cook, stirring constantly, until the mixture coats the back of a spoon, approximately 5 minutes. Do *not* overheat or the mixture will curdle.

3. Remove the mixture to a bowl and blend in the heavy cream and vanilla. Lay a piece of plastic wrap directly on top of the custard mixture to prevent a skin from forming; chill thoroughly.

4. Place the mixture in an ice-cream maker and freeze according to the manufacturer's directions.

This pale blue glass swirl bowl comes from the large collection of my sister-in-law Rita; the grape-motif flatware was made by Rogers in 1881. The homemade quince ice cream is given a perfect finishing touch with a sprinkling of fresh rosemary flowers.

Tarragon Scampi

When I was a New York stockbroker working on Wall Street, I ate once a week at Pietro's Restaurant, which was on Third Avenue and Forty-fifth Street. It was a favorite of several of my clients, who went there to eat the steaks, the lobster fra diavolo, and the lamb chops. I went there for the very good scampi, and when Pietro's ceased to exist, I learned to cook shrimp their way myself; the tarragon scampi in this menu is the result.

The rice dish is a wonderful example of how a recipe passes through cultures, countries, and generations. I learned it from my friend Julia Booth-Clibborn, who got it from her mother, whose friend had had such a dish in North Africa. Like many North African dishes, it calls for all types of nuts and dried fruits, and you can add or omit as you see fit—only be sure to use the real white basmati rice, not the brown, and not regular long grain. (Basmati rice is a flavorful long-grain rice grown in India that has recently become quite popular in this country—so much so that you can even buy Texas-grown basmati-style rice. Indian basmati rice cooks so that the individual grains are dry and separate, very unlike the Japanese or Italian sticky rices; the flavor is nutty and unique.)

The tomato and smoked mozzarella salad requires very ripe and flavorful Italian plum tomatoes, with fresh basil leaves for color and taste. A creamy dressing is a wonderful change from the oil commonly used for this delicious salad.

I like all types of shortcake desserts at all times of the year. The biscuits freeze very well, so when you are making a large amount for breakfast or other meals, make some really pretty ones for dessert. Nectarines are especially good with shortcake—I look for them locally in late summer and for the South American varieties in the spring.

I chose shrimp-pink contemporary pottery to serve this tarragon scampi; the flatware is from a charming Victorian fish service I received as a gift. The waffle-weave tablecloth is exemplary of unconventional table dressing: it's really a large body towel.

M E N U

TARRAGON SCAMPI

BASMATI RICE WITH ALMONDS AND CASHEWS

TOMATO AND SMOKED MOZZARELLA SALAD

NECTARINE SHORTCAKES

Tarragon Scampi

SERVES 4

½ cup olive oil

2 onions, peeled and coarsely grated

4 cloves garlic, peeled and finely minced

1 small bunch fresh tarragon, finely chopped

½ teaspoon salt
Freshly ground black pepper

24 to 32 large shrimp (allow 6 to 8 per person), peeled and deveined
Juice of 1 lemon

1. In a medium skillet, heat olive oil and sauté onions and garlic over medium-low heat for 3 minutes. Add the tarragon, salt, and pepper. Sauté for 1 more minute; do not let the mixture brown. Remove from heat and let cool.

2. In a large bowl, combine the shrimp with the sautéed mixture and fresh lemon juice, stirring until well coated. Let rest at room temperature for 30 minutes.

3. Preheat the broiler. Line a large broiler pan with aluminum foil.

4. Place the shrimps on the foil-lined pan and spoon a generous amount of onion mixture on each. Broil under high heat until the shrimps are pink and the topping is well browned, approximately 4 to 5 minutes. Serve immediately.

Basmati Rice with Almonds and Cashews

SERVES 4 GENEROUSLY

2½ cups basmati rice

3 tablespoons olive or safflower oil

3 potatoes, peeled and sliced ⅛ inch thick

¼ cup unsalted cashews

¼ cup shelled whole almonds

½ thick-skinned orange

5 thin slices fresh ginger

¼ cup golden raisins

12 dried apricots, halved

2 tablespoons drained imported capers

½ teaspoon saffron threads

½ teaspoon cumin seed

½ cup (1 stick) unsalted butter
Salt to taste

1. Carefully wash the rice 5 times to remove the milky coating and starch. Place the washed rice in a large pot of water and let soak for 30 minutes.

2. Heat 2 tablespoons oil in a large, heavy, lidded casserole dish. Carefully layer the potatoes over the oil and cook over low heat for 10 minutes. Do not cook too fast, and do not stir.

3. Drain the rice and parboil in a large pot of salted water for 5 minutes. Drain well.

4. Heat the remaining oil in a small skillet and sauté the cashews and almonds until lightly toasted.

5. With a sharp knife, cut the peel very thinly from the orange, discarding the pith and flesh; cut the peel into nickel-size pieces.

6. Spoon two-thirds of the parboiled rice over the cooked potatoes, being careful not to disturb them. Make small wells over the entire surface of the rice and put small amounts of the nuts, orange peel, ginger, raisins, apricots, and capers separately into each well so that every spoonful of the finished dish will yield a surprise. Cover the fruit and nuts with the remaining rice and sprinkle several pinches of saffron and cumin seed over the top.

7. Melt the butter and pour it over the rice; cover with a wet dishcloth. Place the lid on the casserole and cook over very low heat for 30 minutes. Season with salt and serve immediately.

Tomato and Smoked Mozzarella Salad

SERVES 4

4 large, ripe, firm tomatoes, cut crosswise into ¼-inch slices
1 pound fresh smoked mozzarella, cut into slices ⅛ inch thick
20 fresh basil leaves, torn into small pieces

Creamy Dressing
MAKES 1 CUP
⅔ cup best-quality olive oil
6 tablespoons red wine vinegar
6 tablespoons finely chopped fresh basil (optional)
2 tablespoons heavy cream
Salt and freshly ground black pepper

Arrange the tomato and mozzarella slices in a decorative pattern on individual plates. Garnish with the basil leaves. Whisk the dressing ingredients together in a bowl and spoon over the salad right before serving.

NOTE: If you include chopped basil in the dressing, it should be made right before serving or the fresh herbs will darken.

Nectarine Shortcakes

SERVES 4

8 ripe nectarines
½ cup sugar
⅓ cup heavy cream
⅔ cup Crème Fraîche (page 11)
1 teaspoon vanilla extract
4 large Buttermilk Biscuits (page 188), or 4 (1-inch) slices pound cake

1. Pit and coarsely chop 4 of the nectarines. Mix with ¼ cup sugar in a small bowl and let macerate for at least 30 minutes.

2. Pit and slice the remaining nectarines and set aside.

3. Whip the cream, crème fraîche, remaining ¼ cup sugar, and vanilla to soft peaks.

4. Split the biscuits or pound cake and place one half on each dessert plate. Spoon the macerated nectarines and their juices over the biscuits. Spoon some whipped cream over the nectarines and top with the remaining biscuit half. Place the sliced nectarines over each, top with the remaining whipped cream, and serve.

I love to use potted plants on my tables, especially in early spring, when there is so little in the garden. This late-blooming amaryllis is a really graceful decoration (for some reason, my amaryllis bulbs never grow much above a foot high, so they are the perfect height for table use). The pearl-handled gateau fork, by the way, is from France.

Flank Steak with Coriander Sauce

A good flank steak is very lean, tender, and weighs approximately 1½ pounds. I like to buy steaks this small because I find the grain is fine, and they seem to carve into neater slices. I marinated this flank steak in a simple mixture of Merlot, olive oil, and garlic, then grilled it until rare and sliced it—still hot —into thin strips to serve with large pieces of soft, white, papery flatbread. (I buy a brand called Mid East Bread, which is made by the Ghossain family in Youngstown, Ohio; it is low calorie, very plain but flavorful, and freezes well.)

The peppers are just grilled until the skins blacken, then they are cut in half and dressed with a sherry vinaigrette and lots of flat-leaf Italian parsley. The salad is a combination of thinly sliced radishes, red onion, and fennel, with a dressing of orange juice, oil, and dill. Fennel, by the way, is an unusual and extraordinary vegetable. Listed in most seed catalogues as an herb, it has feathery leaves, like dill, but is anise flavored. The bulbous stem is white and fleshy and very crunchy. It is appetizing and refreshing, excellent raw, in salads, or cooked—braised or sautéed. (It is interesting to note that fennel has almost no calories and almost no nutritive value.)

This pink grapefruit sorbet is sweet, sour, and delectable. I first tasted it in Palm Beach at the home of a friend; her chef made both white and pink sorbets using white and red grapefruit and served them in round scoops on top of caramelized sugar "doilies." Even without the doilies, though, this is a beautiful dessert.

The table setting for this flank steak with coriander sauce was truly a combined effort: the tablecloth is a cotton flour sack embroidered by one of my seminar students with the Three Little Pigs; my assistant Amanda lent the green and white dinerware plates and the green-Bakelite–handled flatware, while my sister Laura contributed the piggy-decorated Depression glasses. The green and white napkins are my own.

M E N U

FLANK STEAK WITH CORIANDER SAUCE
SALAD WITH RADISH, FENNEL, AND RED ONION
GRILLED PEPPERS
GRAPEFRUIT SORBET

Flank Steak with Coriander Sauce

SERVES 3 TO 4

1½ pounds flank steak
2 cloves garlic, peeled and thinly sliced lengthwise
2 tablespoons olive oil
½ cup dry red wine, preferably Merlot
2 loaves fresh flatbread, warmed in the oven

Coriander Sauce
1 cup coarsely chopped fresh coriander (cilantro)
⅓ cup olive oil
1 tablespoon very finely minced red onion
Salt and freshly ground black pepper

1. Place the flank steak in a large dish. Combine the garlic, olive oil, and wine and pour over the meat. Let marinate at room temperature for at least 30 minutes or overnight in the refrigerator.

2. Combine all ingredients for the sauce, season to taste, and let sit at room temperature for at least 30 minutes.

3. Prepare the grill.

4. Remove the meat from the marinade and grill over hot coals until done to your liking (about 10 minutes for rare), turning the meat once while cooking.

5. Remove the meat from the grill and slice diagonally, against the grain.

6. To serve, place half a warmed flatbread on each plate and cover with overlapping slices of meat. Drizzle with the coriander sauce.

Salad with Radish, Fennel, and Red Onion

SERVES 3 TO 4

1 small head green leaf lettuce
1 small bunch red radishes, trimmed, cleaned, and thinly sliced
1 small bulb fennel, trimmed, cleaned, and thinly sliced crosswise
1 red onion, peeled and thinly sliced crosswise

Dressing
MAKES APPROXIMATELY ½ CUP
Juice of 1 orange
1 tablespoon olive oil
½ tablespoon chopped fresh dill
Salt and freshly ground black pepper

Tear the lettuce leaves into bite-size pieces and place in a serving bowl with the radishes, fennel, and red onion. Whisk together the dressing ingredients and toss with the salad right before serving.

Grilled Peppers

SERVES 3 TO 4

3 tablespoons olive oil
1½ tablespoons sherry wine vinegar
Salt and freshly ground black pepper
1 red bell pepper
1 green bell pepper
1 yellow bell pepper
2 tablespoons coarsely chopped fresh flat Italian parsley

1. In a small bowl, whisk together the oil and vinegar and season to taste. Set aside.

2. Grill the peppers over hot coals until the skins are blackened and the peppers are tender, 15 to 20 minutes. Be sure to

turn the peppers frequently so that they cook evenly on all sides.

3. Remove the peppers from the grill, halve them, and cut out the seeds. Drizzle with the oil and vinegar mixture and sprinkle with parsley. Serve immediately.

Grapefruit Sorbet

MAKES 1 GENEROUS QUART

5 *small or 4 large red grapefruit,*
   preferably Indian River or Marsh
   Ruby
1 *cup sugar*
¼ *cup Champagne, flat or bubbly*

1. Finely grate the peel of 1 grapefruit into a medium bowl and set aside. Juice grapefruit (you should have 4 cups of juice). Strain the juice into the bowl along with the grated peel. (Using a wooden spoon, push as much juice and pulp through the sieve as possible.)

2. Put the sugar in a noncorroding saucepan and stir in 1 cup of the strained juice. Heat the mixture over medium heat, stirring constantly, until the sugar dissolves. Do not let the mixture boil.

3. Blend the sugar mixture into the remaining grapefruit juice, add the Champagne, and chill thoroughly. Freeze the mixture in an ice-cream maker according to the manufacturer's directions.

4. Serve the sorbet with sections of fresh grapefruit. A little bubbly Champagne can also be poured over the sorbet if desired.

NOTE: This sorbet can also be made with pink or white grapefruit.

The Marsh Ruby grapefruits served with this grapefruit sorbet are such a wonderful color they should be set off, as here, by a simple white bowl.

Sautéed Boudin Noir

I was first introduced to boudin, a soft, fresh-made sausage, by Paul Prud-homme, the great New Orleans chef. I was writing an article on Cajun cooking and accompanied him on a trip to the Louisiana swamps. One Saturday morning, driving across a levee, we stopped at a little shack of a restaurant, where Paul told me to try the *boudin noir*—the blood sausage. It reminded me a little of Polish blood sausage, although that has a much coarser texture. Boudin noir is delicate, tender, spicy, and herb-flecked; the filling is smooth but slightly dense. Great care must be taken to sauté or poach the sausages gently so the casing doesn't burst; the twists must also be left uncut until after cooking or the filling may leak out.

I serve boudin noir with lots of French bread, a sauté of kohlrabi and apples, and simple okra stew. For the uninitiated, kohlrabi is a hard green or purple knob of a vegetable that grows above ground. The bulb has turniplike leaves and a very mild, sweet turniplike flavor. It is excellent served raw, thinly sliced, or steamed or sautéed until tender.

Hazelnut ice cream, with a crunchy topping of pulverized praline candy, is a special treat and a fitting end to this simple meal. The hazelnuts are first roasted, then cleaned of their skins. I find that by rubbing the warm nuts in a large Turkish towel I can remove most of the skins quickly and easily. It is very important to roast the nuts to bring out their true flavor—just be careful not to scorch them.

Do remember that the table setting must complement the atmosphere of a menu as well as the color and texture of the individual dishes. Sautéed boudin with kohlrabi and apples and a simple okra stew make up a country meal; this unusual, square wooden breadboard is the perfect rustic plate. The table runner, embroidered in a complex cross-stitch, is from Yugoslavia.

MENU

SAUTÉED BOUDIN NOIR
SAUTÉED KOHLRABI AND APPLES
SIMPLE OKRA STEW
HAZELNUT ICE CREAM WITH PRALINE TOPPING

Sautéed Boudin Noir

SERVES 6

6 boudin noir (*black blood sausages*)
3 tablespoons unsalted butter
¼ cup Calvados

1. In a large skillet, sauté the sausages in the butter over medium heat for 5 minutes.

2. Add the Calvados to the pan and lower the heat so that the sausages do not burst while cooking. Cook 15 minutes. Serve immediately with a bit of sauce from the pan.

Sautéed Kohlrabi and Apples

SERVES 6

4 tablespoons (½ stick) unsalted butter
4 small kohlrabi, peeled and cut into
    ¼-inch slices
1 Granny Smith apple, halved, seeded,
    and cut into thin wedges

1. Melt 2 tablespoons butter in a large skillet and sauté the kohlrabi slices until they are bright green, approximately 5 minutes.

2. In a separate skillet, sauté the apple in the remaining butter until slightly browned and barely softened, about 5 minutes. Toss with the warm kohlrabi and serve immediately.

Simple Okra Stew

SERVES 6

1 pound small fresh okra
1 large onion, peeled and sliced
3 tablespoons unsalted butter
½ teaspoon ground cumin
2 ripe tomatoes, coarsely chopped
    Salt and freshly ground black pepper

1. Blanch the okra in a large pot of boiling water until tender, approximately 4 to 5 minutes. Drain well.

2. In a large skillet, sauté the onion in the butter with the cumin until softened, about 5 minutes; do not brown. Stir in the okra and chopped tomatoes and season to taste; simmer for 10 minutes. Serve hot.

Hazelnut Ice Cream with Praline Topping

MAKES 2 PINTS

3 egg yolks
½ cup sugar
1½ cups milk, scalded
1 cup heavy cream
1 cup roasted and skinned hazelnuts
    (see Note), finely ground

Praline
½ cup sugar
2 tablespoons water
⅜ cup roasted and skinned hazelnuts
    (see Note)

1. To make the ice cream, whisk together the egg yolks and sugar in a medium saucepan until blended. Slowly add the scalded milk, whisking constantly, then place the saucepan over low heat. Cook the mixture (stirring constantly so the eggs don't curdle) until it coats the back of a spoon, about 10 minutes. Remove the mixture to a bowl, place a piece of plastic wrap directly on top of the custard, and chill thoroughly.

2. Whip the cream to soft peaks and fold it into the well-chilled custard. Gently fold in the ground hazelnuts, place the mixture in an ice-cream maker, and freeze according to the manufacturer's directions.

3. To make the praline, combine the sugar and water in a small, heavy saucepan and bring to a boil. Do not stir. Cook over medium-high heat until the mixture becomes dark caramel in color, about 5 minutes longer. Add the nuts.

4. Pour mixture onto a piece of parchment paper; let cool and harden.

5. Break the praline into small pieces and pulverize them in a food processor. (The praline will keep indefinitely, tightly sealed, in a cool, dry place.)

6. Serve the ice cream with a sprinkling of ground praline over the top.

NOTE: To prepare the hazelnuts, roast them in a preheated 300° F. oven until nicely browned, about 15 minutes. Place immediately in a kitchen towel (Turkish toweling is best) and rub them to remove the skins.

Ice cream, here our homemade hazelnut flavor, always looks prettier with a little topping for color and texture; I used praline, a classic crushed nut caramel. The deep blue plate is another piece of our favorite cobalt-blue Depression glass.

Crab Bisque

I first tasted ratatouille in a little Provencal restaurant in Paris near the church of St. Sulpice. I had ordered an omelette, and it was served with a side dish of beautiful summer vegetables—zucchini, peppers, eggplant, onions, and tomatoes—stewed in an infusion of rich olive oil, garlic, thyme, and marjoram. I asked the waiter how the dish was cooked; he brought the chef, who told me that the secret was to cook each vegetable separately first, then to layer them and continue cooking just enough to get all the flavors to intermingle. Most important, he said, was to maintain the individual flavors of each vegetable.

Now that we have all the wonderful colored peppers available, with fresh herbs and special olive oils, we can almost make such a ratatouille at home. I, of course, like to make it in the summertime, when the ingredients can be picked fresh from the garden; it is a wonderful, colorful dish to make en masse for a large crowd. If I have leftovers, though, I don't freeze them: I find that the vegetables become soggy and lifeless.

Begin the meal with a large bowl of crab bisque. This is so easy to make and so very good, but it is rich, so the rest of the menu should be as we state it—vegetables and a really tasty bottom-crust plum crumble for dessert. The cinnamon, almond, and vanilla flavoring gives the crumble a uniqueness that your guests will love. You can substitute vanilla-flavored, slightly sweetened sour cream for the heavy cream, or just dollops of crème fraîche.

Like so many others, I do love antique linens and laces—but I also have a weakness for the vivid colors and funny motifs of 1950s fabrics. The fruit-patterned tablecloth beneath the green Harlequin plates picks up the bright colors of the ratatouille in this menu; the green Depression glass champagne flute and red and yellow Bakelite-handled flatware carry on the summery color scheme.

M E N U

CRAB BISQUE

RATATOUILLE

GREEN SALAD WITH GINGER-LIME DRESSING

BOTTOM-CRUST PLUM CRUMBLE

Crab Bisque

SERVES 6

5 or 6 scallions, white and green parts finely chopped crosswise
4 tablespoons (½ stick) unsalted butter, cut into small pieces
¼ cup all-purpose flour
3 cups milk
1½ cups heavy cream
2 teaspoons salt
½ teaspoon ground mace
½ teaspoon paprika
Tabasco
1 pound lump crabmeat, picked over for shell and cartilage

1. In a large, deep kettle, sauté the scallions in the melted butter until softened, 3 to 4 minutes. Blend in the flour and cook over low heat for 5 minutes.

2. Stir in the milk and cream and cook just until warm.

3. Stir the spices and Tabasco to taste into the soup mixture, blending well. Add the crabmeat but do not stir or the crabmeat may break into small pieces. Heat gently (do not let boil) and serve.

Ratatouille

SERVES 6 GENEROUSLY

½ cup olive oil
2 onions, peeled and chopped
4 cloves garlic, peeled and left whole
1 large eggplant, cut into 1-inch cubes
1 large zucchini, cut into ½-inch slices
8 ripe, firm plum tomatoes, seeded and cut into eighths
1 red bell pepper, seeded and cut into ½-inch squares
1 green bell pepper, seeded and cut into ½-inch squares
½ yellow bell pepper, seeded and julienned

Several sprigs of fresh marjoram and thyme
Salt and freshly ground black pepper

1. In a large, flameproof casserole or lidded skillet, heat 3 tablespoons of the olive oil. Gently sauté the onions and garlic until soft, about 5 minutes. Remove from the casserole with a slotted spoon and set aside.

2. Add more oil to the casserole if necessary. Sauté the eggplant cubes over medium heat just until soft, approximately 5 minutes. Remove from the casserole. Continue to cook the remaining vegetables separately in the casserole, adding additional oil when necessary and sautéing just until the vegetables begin to soften.

3. When all the vegetables have been sautéed, layer them in the casserole, distributing the herb sprigs among them. Season to taste. Cover the entire mixture with a sheet of parchment paper and the casserole or skillet lid. Cook over low heat until all the vegetables are tender but not mushy, about 20 minutes. Serve hot, warm, or cold.

Green Salad with Ginger-Lime Dressing

SERVES 6

1 head green leaf lettuce, torn into bite-size pieces
1 ripe nectarine, very thinly sliced
2 tablespoons fresh curly parsley, torn into small pieces

Ginger-Lime Dressing
MAKES ¾ CUP
6 tablespoons olive oil
Juice of 1½ limes
1½ teaspoons honey
1½ tablespoons grated fresh ginger
Salt and freshly ground black pepper

Combine the lettuce, nectarine slices, and parsley in a large bowl. Whisk the dressing ingredients together and toss with the salad right before serving.

Bottom-Crust Plum Crumble

SERVES 6 TO 8

1¼ cups plus 2 tablespoons sugar
¼ teaspoon salt
½ cup (1 stick) unsalted butter, chilled and cut into small pieces
1¼ cups all-purpose flour
¾ teaspoon ground cinnamon
¼ teaspoon baking powder
2 eggs
½ cup heavy cream
1½ teaspoons almond extract
½ teaspoon vanilla extract
1½ pounds (approximately 12) dark plums, pitted and cut into eighths
    Heavy cream, whipped to soft peaks

1. Preheat the oven to 350° F.

2. In a medium bowl, combine 1 cup sugar and the salt; cut in the butter until the mixture resembles coarse meal. Stir in the flour.

3. Set aside half the mixture. Add the cinnamon, baking powder, and 1 egg to the other half. Mix until well blended. Press into the bottom of a 9-inch tart pan. Bake for 10 minutes.

4. While the pastry is baking, whisk together ¼ cup of the sugar, the remaining egg, the cream, and the almond and vanilla extracts.

5. Remove the pastry from the oven and spread the plum slices on top. Pour the cream mixture over the fruit and sprinkle with the reserved butter-flour mixture. Sprinkle with the remaining 2 tablespoons sugar and bake until the crumb topping is nicely browned and the fruit tender, 20 to 30 minutes. Serve warm or cold with whipped cream.

These ranunculuses echo the colors in the tablecloth and in the fruit-patterned napkin (which is really a dishtowel); their informal air is just right for the plum crumble dessert.

Barbecued Mussels and Clams

The scent of food cooking on an outdoor grill always reminds me of summer: hot, healthy days seem to end with a barbecue on the beach or in the garden. But the need to reduce fat in our diets—and our new pride in American cooking—has made the grill an important part of everyday life, and now I find myself lighting up the coals almost all year around. (Fortunately, manufacturers are coming up with grills that can safely be used on sheltered porches, or even right indoors.)

The clams and mussels in this menu could conceivably be cooked in the oven, although they would then lack the special flavor imparted by a charcoal fire. The tomato-caper topping is excellent, and the shellfish can be served hot right off the grill, or even cold.

The side dish of brown basmati rice, crunchy whole-wheat berries, and finely diced sautéed vegetables could easily grace any vegetarian table. The salad is a personalized version of the Caesar salad we all love. I particularly enjoy making it at the end of the summer when the heads of romaine lettuce in the garden attain gargantuan proportions.

Sunrise Sherbet is based on a favorite childhood pastime. We often doctored canned fruit juices with lemon or lime juice, coconut milk, mashed bananas, or strawberries, and froze our concoctions in ice-cube trays or metal tumblers. We would chop away at these sorbets with sharp forks—delicious, healthy fun. Here it's even better with these superb pecan cookies.

The colors and textures of these dishes—barbecued mussels and clams and basmati rice with whole-wheat berries—are so interesting, I chose to present them on clear Depression glass Manhattan-pattern plates. The green and white print cloth and napkins were a happy coincidence: they were found separately and complement each other and the green-painted Lloyd loom chairs.

M E N U

ROMAINE SALAD WITH GARLIC-HERB CROUTONS
BARBECUED MUSSELS AND CLAMS
BROWN BASMATI RICE WITH WHOLE-WHEAT BERRIES
SUNRISE SHERBET
PECAN COOKIES

Romaine Salad with Garlic-Herb Croutons

Garlic-Herb Croutons
- 1 clove garlic, peeled and very finely minced
- 1 tablespoon chopped fresh flat Italian parsley
- ½ tablespoon chopped fresh marjoram
- 1 tablespoon chopped fresh basil
- 1 teaspoon chopped fresh oregano
- ½ cup olive oil, plus extra for sautéing
- 8 (¼-inch-thick) slices French bread, cut into fourths

Dressing
MAKES ¾ CUP
- 3 cloves garlic, peeled and very finely minced
- 1 egg yolk
- 2 to 3 tablespoons red wine vinegar, or to taste
- ⅓ cup olive oil
- 1 tablespoon Dijon mustard
- 3 anchovy fillets, drained and chopped
- ⅓ cup freshly grated Parmesan cheese
  Freshly ground black pepper

- 1 handful of coarsely cut romaine lettuce leaves per person

1. To make the croutons, whisk together all the ingredients except the bread slices. Brush both sides of each bread slice with a bit of this mixture and sauté in a bit of olive oil over low heat until crisp and lightly browned. Let cool completely.

2. Whisk all dressing ingredients together until well blended.

3. Right before serving, place the lettuce in a large bowl and toss with the dressing. Add the croutons and toss again.

Barbecued Mussels and Clams

Tomato-Caper Sauce
MAKES ABOUT 1½ CUPS
- 1 onion, peeled and finely chopped
- ¼ cup olive oil
- 8 ripe plum tomatoes or 4 large tomatoes, coarsely chopped
- 2 tablespoons drained imported capers
- ½ cup chopped fresh basil, coriander (cilantro), and/or flat Italian parsley
- ½ cup dry white wine
  Salt and freshly ground black pepper

- 8 to 10 mussels per person, well washed and scrubbed
- 3 to 4 large cherrystone clams per person, well washed and scrubbed

1. To make the sauce, sauté the onion in olive oil until soft but not browned, about 5 minutes. Add the chopped tomatoes and cook until soft, about 2 minutes. Stir in the capers, chopped herbs, and wine and season to taste. Set aside.

2. Grill the mussels and clams over very hot coals until the shells open; the mussels will take 1 or 2 minutes and the clams approximately 3 minutes. Pry off one side of each bivalve and discard. Spoon a bit of topping on each and heat till bubbly, 3 to 5 minutes longer. Serve hot or cold.

Brown Basmati Rice with Whole-Wheat Berries

- 1 tablespoon unsalted butter
- 2 cups brown basmati rice (available at gourmet and health-food stores)
- 1 cup whole-wheat berries

5 cups water
Zest of 1½ lemons
2 tablespoons olive oil
3 scallions, white and green parts very thinly sliced
1 rib celery, cut into ¼-inch dice
½ red bell pepper, cut into ¼-inch squares
½ yellow bell pepper, cut into ¼-inch squares
½ cubanelle (or green bell) pepper, cut into ¼-inch squares
2 tablespoons fresh lemon juice
¼ cup safflower oil
Salt and freshly ground black pepper

1. In a large saucepan, heat the butter and sauté the rice for 3 minutes. Add the whole-wheat berries, water, and zest of 1 lemon. Simmer, covered, until the rice and wheat berries are tender but still crunchy and the water has been absorbed, about 20 to 30 minutes. Remove from the heat, drain, and let cool.

2. In a medium skillet, heat the olive oil and sauté all the chopped vegetables over medium heat for 3 minutes. Let cool slightly.

3. Combine the rice and wheat berries with the sautéed vegetables in a large serving bowl. Add the lemon juice, safflower oil, and remaining lemon zest; season to taste and toss well. Serve at room temperature.

Sunrise Sherbet

MAKES APPROXIMATELY 1½ PINTS

2 cups peach or apricot nectar
2 tablespoons fresh lime juice
⅓ cup sweetened condensed milk

Combine the ingredients; freeze the mixture in an ice-cream maker according to the manufacturer's directions. Serve with a pecan cookie.

Pecan Cookies

MAKES 30 TO 36 COOKIES

1½ cups all-purpose flour
¼ teaspoon baking powder
¼ teaspoon baking soda
½ cup (1 stick) unsalted butter
½ cup granulated sugar
½ cup dark brown sugar, loosely packed
1 egg
1½ teaspoons vanilla extract
¾ cup finely chopped pecans
36 pecan halves

1. Sift together the flour, baking powder, and baking soda; set aside.

2. Cream the butter and sugars until light and fluffy. Beat in the egg and vanilla. Gradually add the flour mixture, a bit at a time, until thoroughly blended. Stir in the chopped pecans.

3. Shape the dough into an even cylinder approximately 1½ inches in diameter. Wrap in plastic wrap and chill for at least 15 minutes.

4. Preheat the oven to 350° F. Line a baking sheet with parchment paper or lightly butter it.

5. Remove the plastic wrap and cut the dough into slices approximately ¼ inch thick. Place the slices on the baking sheet (leave room for them to spread) and lightly press a pecan half into the center of each. Bake until lightly browned, about 12 minutes. Let cool and serve with Sunrise Sherbet.

This glass was probably designed for cocktails, but it works well as a dish for my Sunrise Sherbet. The spoon is Rogers fiddle-pattern plate, made in 1847.

Filet of Beef with Red Pepper Butter

Although filet of beef is one of the most expensive cuts at the meat counter, I find that it is really an economical purchase when entertaining because one thick slice or tournedos is sufficient for almost everyone. After trimming the filet I roast or grill it whole, plain or stuffed, or I cut it into 1½- or 2-inch-thick slices that I broil or grill; these individual steaks are so delicious, all they need for flavoring is a simple red pepper butter.

Sweet potatoes are a very good and nutritious vegetable, and one of my favorites; if I'm eating alone, I often just bake a sweet potato and eat it with a salad. For the sautéed version in this menu, parboil the potatoes, peel them, and sauté thick slices in melted butter with thyme.

The julienne of zucchini and summer squash is easy to prepare if you have a mandoline, but the vegetables can also be julienned by hand using a Japanese cleaver. The salad of crunchy daikon radish and slightly bitter chicory tastes good with a dressing flavored with fresh, sweet pear.

A bowl of fresh fruit sprinkled with liqueur is the classic Quick Cook dessert: simple, pretty, and so easy. In this case, we used framboise to enhance the berries.

By now you will have realized how fond I am of the color green and will appreciate how pleased I was to find these 1940s square Fire King plates and this flatware with its green-painted wooden handles. They provide a nice, solid background for the filet of beef and sweet potato slices.

MENU

FILET OF BEEF WITH RED PEPPER BUTTER
SWEET POTATO SLICES WITH THYME
JULIENNE OF ZUCCHINI AND SUMMER SQUASH
CHICORY AND DAIKON SALAD WITH PEAR DRESSING
BERRIES WITH FRAMBOISE

Filet of Beef with Red Pepper Butter

SERVES 4

Red Pepper Butter
½ *small red bell pepper, seeded and finely minced*
4 *tablespoons (½ stick) unsalted butter, at room temperature*
Pinch of cayenne pepper
Salt to taste

4 *beef filets, 1½ to 2 inches thick*

1. In a small bowl, combine all ingredients for the red pepper butter by hand until thoroughly mixed. Refrigerate until ready to use.

2. Preheat the broiler.

3. Broil the filets for 6 minutes. Turn them over and top each with approximately ½ tablespoon red pepper butter. Return to the broiler and cook to desired degree of doneness, 6 to 9 minutes longer.

4. Remove the filets from the broiler and top with another ½ tablespoon of red pepper butter. Return to the broiler just long enough to melt the butter. Serve hot.

Sweet Potato Slices with Thyme

SERVES 4

3 medium sweet potatoes
2 tablespoons (¼ stick) unsalted butter
1 teaspoon fresh thyme leaves
   Salt and freshly ground black pepper

1. Boil the sweet potatoes in a large pot of water until tender, approximately 15 minutes. Drain well.

2. While the potatoes are still warm, peel with a sharp paring knife and cut into ½-inch diagonal slices.

3. In a large skillet, melt the butter and add the thyme. Sauté the potatoes until they are hot and the edges are nicely browned. Season to taste and serve.

Julienne of Zucchini and Summer Squash

SERVES 4

2 small zucchini
1 small yellow summer squash
2 tablespoons (¼ stick) unsalted butter
1 large sprig fresh rosemary
   Salt and freshly ground black pepper

1. Cut all the squash into 2½-inch lengths and, using a mandoline slicer, julienne each piece lengthwise, discarding the seed core.

2. Melt the butter in a medium skillet and add the rosemary and squash. Sauté until the squash is just softened, 3 to 5 minutes. Season to taste and serve.

Chicory and Daikon Salad with Pear Dressing

SERVES 4

1 handful of curly chicory per person
1 (6-inch) piece daikon (Japanese white radish)

Pear Dressing
MAKES APPROXIMATELY ½ CUP
½ ripe pear, peeled, cored, and cut into small chunks
1 teaspoon lemon juice
1 tablespoon safflower oil
   Salt and freshly ground black pepper

1. Place the chicory in a serving bowl.

2. Peel the daikon with a vegetable peeler and, still using the peeler, slice the radish into long, thin "ribbons." Add to the chicory.

3. To make the dressing, liquefy the pear by pushing it through a sieve with a wooden spoon into a small bowl. Stir in the lemon juice and oil, season to taste, and toss with the salad.

Berries with Framboise

SERVES 4

½ pint ripe blackberries
½ pint ripe red raspberries
½ pint blueberries
1 tablespoon framboise (raspberry liqueur)

1. Gently toss the berries together in a serving bowl.

2. Sprinkle with the liqueur and serve.

Grilled Swordfish Steaks with Chervil Butter

A good soup can make any simple meal a success. This carrot soup is my daughter Alexis's favorite; she serves it hot in the winter and cold in the summer. I find that the flavor of the carrots is greatly enhanced by adding a parsnip or a leek or even a ripe pear or apple to the soup while it is simmering. The garnish can be more chopped fresh coriander, or better yet the small flowers from the coriander plant. The flowers of herbs have the essence of their flavor, often without the strong pungency of the herbs themselves.

I don't know anyone who does not enjoy grilled swordfish. Buy steaks that are at least an inch thick, and be sure to marinate them in lemon juice or grapefruit juice with olive oil for 30 minutes or more. Always grill fish over very hot coals and take care that the grill is clean and well oiled before placing the fish on it. If the grill is well prepared, the final appearance of the fish will be perfect, with strong grill marks decorating the firm flesh of the steaks. During grilling, rotate the steaks one quarter turn to achieve a crisscross pattern, if you desire.

Baked fruits, especially apricots, are to me one of the most desirable desserts. A gentle baking in a buttered and sugared dish, with a bit of rich cream added at the last minute, can produce the most delectable concoction. The fruit should be perfectly ripe, the butter sweet, and the sugar scented with rose-geranium leaves, vanilla bean, or even a piece of fragrant lemon peel. I keep several varieties of scented sugars in jars in my pantry—they keep forever and are handy to use in pies, in baked desserts, or with poached fruits.

This menu of carrot soup and swordfish steaks was served on pink lace-pattern Depression glass plates that have, despite their delicate appearance, survived very well —they were made in 1935 by the Hocking Glass Company.

M E N U

CARROT SOUP WITH CORIANDER AND CHIVES
CUCUMBER SALAD
GRILLED SWORDFISH STEAKS WITH CHERVIL BUTTER
TWICE-COOKED POTATOES
BAKED APRICOTS WITH ROSE-GERANIUM SUGAR

Carrot Soup with Coriander and Chives

SERVES 4

4 tablespoons (½ stick) unsalted butter
1 shallot, peeled and minced
1½ teaspoons ground coriander
4 cups Chicken Stock (page 13)
1½ pounds carrots, peeled and thinly sliced
1 large parsnip, peeled and thinly sliced (optional)
½ cup heavy cream
Salt and freshly ground black pepper
1½ tablespoons chopped fresh coriander (cilantro)
Fresh chives

1. Melt the butter in a heavy saucepan. Add the shallot and sprinkle with the ground coriander. Sauté for 2 minutes, stirring frequently.

2. Add stock, carrots, and parsnip. Bring to a boil, reduce heat, and simmer, covered, until vegetables are tender, 35 minutes.

3. Process the mixture in 2-cup batches in a food processor until smooth.

4. Return mixture to the saucepan, add the cream, and heat through. Season to taste, then serve hot or cold, garnished with fresh coriander and fresh chives.

Cucumber Salad

SERVES 4

Dressing
MAKES ¾ CUP

1 teaspoon crushed fresh rosemary leaves
¼ cup balsamic vinegar
¼ cup olive oil
¼ cup safflower oil
2 tablespoons Dijon mustard
Salt and freshly ground black pepper
Pinch of sugar

2 long seedless cucumbers (or 6 to 8 Kirby cucumbers), washed and very thinly sliced

1. In a small skillet, gently heat the crushed rosemary and vinegar over low heat for 2 minutes. (This accentuates the flavor of the rosemary.) Pour into a large bowl, add the remaining dressing ingredients, and whisk until thick and thoroughly combined.

2. Add the sliced cucumbers to the bowl and toss well. Refrigerate until ready to serve.

Grilled Swordfish Steaks with Chervil Butter

SERVES 4

2 pounds swordfish, cut into 1- to 1½-inch steaks
¼ cup olive oil
Juice of 1 lemon

Chervil Butter
½ cup (1 stick) unsalted butter, at room temperature
½ cup chopped fresh chervil
Salt and freshly ground black pepper

1. Brush the swordfish with the olive oil and lemon juice. Let stand at room temperature for at least 30 minutes. Meanwhile, prepare the grill.

2. Combine ingredients for the chervil butter in a small bowl and mix thoroughly. Set aside.

3. Cook the fish over hot coals, to which mesquite wood chips or mesquite charcoal has been added for extra flavor. (Be sure to spray grill with vege-

table oil to prevent sticking.) Grill for 7 to 10 minutes, turning once.

4. Remove fish from the grill, place on a heated serving platter, and brush with the softened chervil butter.

Twice-cooked Potatoes

SERVES 4

16 red- or white-skinned new potatoes, quartered
3 tablespoons unsalted butter
¼ cup fresh chervil leaves
    Salt and freshly ground black pepper

1. Cook the potatoes in boiling water until tender; small potatoes will take approximately 10 minutes. Drain well.

2. Melt the butter in a large skillet, add the boiled potatoes, and sauté over medium heat just until crispy, about 5 minutes. Sprinkle with chervil, season to taste, and serve hot.

Baked Apricots with Rose-Geranium Sugar

SERVES 4

4 tablespoons (½ stick) unsalted butter, at room temperature
½ cup rose-geranium sugar (see Note)
8 ripe apricots, halved and pitted
½ cup heavy cream

1. Preheat oven to 375° F. Use half the butter and rose-geranium sugar to butter and sugar a large baking dish.

2. Place the halved apricots, cut side down, on top of the butter and sugar. Dot with the remaining butter and sprinkle with the remaining sugar. Bake for 15 minutes. Remove from the oven

and pour the cream around the fruit; return to the oven for 5 minutes. Serve hot or warm.

NOTE: To make rose-geranium sugar, mix 1 cup granulated sugar with 8 rose-geranium leaves. Store in a tightly covered jar for at least 1 week. The sugar can be used in many desserts, in teas, and for flavoring whipped cream.

The apricots were baked in this French porcelain dish and served on more lace-pattern glass; the pink cotton damask tablecloth and napkins are from the collection of my sister Laura.

Red-Hot Chicken

While on a trip to the island of St.-Barthélemy in the Caribbean, I became an avid fan of the Scotch Bonnet, a tiny, pretty red, yellow, or orange pepper with thin, burning-hot flesh. Scotch Bonnets are used in West Indian cooking to flavor vinegar and oils; pickled, they are served as a relish with lentil and kidney bean salads and as a chutney for grilled fishes and meats. I brought some home from the island (they are also available here in West Indian food stores) and used them in a marinade for this red-hot chicken recipe. The flavor does mellow a bit when the peppers are cooked—but be cautious when using such a powerful ingredient.

The red pepper flake pasta continues the spicy theme of this dinner menu; use more or less pepper according to your own palate and those of your guests. The herb sauce should just coat the pasta—use enough to enhance the flavor of the freshly made fettuccine, not overwhelm it.

The electric slicer has become an indispensable appliance for my style of cooking. With it I can slice apples paper-thin for puff pastry tarts, onions for soup, tomatoes for salad, potatoes for pommes Anna, and the long, thin slices of eggplant for this menu. A very sharp knife can of course accomplish the same task, but the time involved will be much greater.

Each year I make a point of driving to Maine during the last part of August, when the wild blueberries are in season. I pick my own if I have time, or I buy as many quarts as I can find for preserves and sauces and to freeze whole for use during the rest of the year. Everything tastes especially good when made with these tiny, flavorful berries—they make excellent pies, cobblers, cakes, and pancakes. This sauce is very good with fresh strawberries, peaches, or over vanilla ice cream. By adding a bit of blackberry liqueur, if you like, just a bit more interest is created in the flavor.

MENU

RED-HOT CHICKEN
RED PEPPER FLAKE PASTA WITH HERB SAUCE
GRILLED EGGPLANT
ASPARAGUS WITH RED ONION
STRAWBERRIES WITH WILD BLUEBERRY SAUCE

When marinating meat or fish, always use a noncorroding bowl or dish, like the pottery baking dish that holds these chicken breasts in their red-hot marinade of peppers and citrus juices.

Red-Hot Chicken

SERVES 4

2 tablespoons olive oil
Juice of 1 lemon
Juice of 1 lime
Pinch of freshly ground black pepper
1 Scotch Bonnet chile, very thinly sliced, with seeds removed
2 teaspoons chopped fresh flat Italian parsley leaves
4 whole chicken breasts

1. Combine all ingredients except the chicken in a baking dish. Add the chicken and marinate for 30 minutes.

2. Remove the chicken from the marinade. Reserve chile and parsley leaves. Cook chicken skin side down on a grill over hot coals (or under a very hot broiler) until nicely browned, 6 to 8 minutes. Turn over and continue cooking for 10 to 12 minutes, until chicken is done. Serve immediately, garnished with the reserved chile slices and parsley from the marinade.

NOTE: Scotch Bonnets are grown in the Caribbean and Mexico. Any small, very hot red chile can be substituted if Scotch Bonnets are not available.

Red Pepper Flake Pasta with Herb Sauce

SERVES 4 GENEROUSLY

Pasta
3½ cups all-purpose flour
1 teaspoon salt
5 eggs
1 tablespoon olive oil
1 teaspoon crumbled red pepper flakes

Herb Sauce
⅓ cup extra-virgin (green) olive oil
1 tablespoon fresh marjoram leaves
1 teaspoon chopped fresh sage leaves
1 tablespoon chopped fresh curly parsley

Salt and freshly ground black pepper
Freshly grated Parmesan cheese

1. To make the pasta, combine the flour and salt on a large board. Make a well in the center and break the eggs into it; add the olive oil and red pepper flakes. Gently mix all ingredients with a fork, then knead the dough with the heels of your hands until smooth, about 5 minutes. (If the dough seems sticky, add a little more flour.)

2. Roll the dough to the desired thickness with a pasta machine, following the manufacturer's directions. Set the machine to fettuccine width and pass the dough sheet through it. Wrap and store in the freezer until ready to use.

3. Mix all ingredients for the sauce and set aside.

4. Cook the pasta in a large pot of boiling water just until tender, 3 to 5 minutes. Drain well.

5. Toss the cooked pasta with the herb sauce and season with salt and pepper. Serve with freshly grated Parmesan.

Grilled Eggplant

SERVES 4

2 small Japanese eggplants, trimmed and thinly sliced lengthwise
2 tablespoons olive oil
Salt and freshly ground black pepper

1. Brush slices of eggplant with olive oil and season with salt and pepper.

2. Grill over very hot coals or under broiler until tender, 2 to 3 minutes on each side. Serve immediately.

Asparagus with Red Onion

SERVES 4

Dressing
MAKES ½ CUP
  ¼ cup olive oil
  1 tablespoon rice wine vinegar
  1 tablespoon heavy cream
  1 tablespoon Dijon mustard
  1 egg yolk
     Pinch of salt

  1 pound thick asparagus, trimmed and
     cut into 1-inch lengths
  ½ red onion, peeled and diced

1. To make the dressing, whisk all ingredients together until creamy.

2. In a large pot of boiling water, cook the asparagus until just tender, 3 to 4 minutes. Drain and plunge immediately into ice water to stop the cooking process. Drain well.

3. Toss the asparagus with the vinaigrette and arrange on a serving platter. Sprinkle the red onion on top and serve immediately.

Strawberries with Wild Blueberry Sauce

SERVES 4

Sauce
  ¾ cup fresh or frozen wild blueberries
  1 cup sugar
  2 tablespoons blackberry liqueur

  1 quart ripe red strawberries, hulled
     and halved
     Fresh mint leaves

1. To make the sauce, combine the blueberries and sugar in a heavy saucepan. Simmer the mixture over low heat for 5 minutes; the blueberries should remain whole. Remove from the heat and stir in the liqueur. Chill until ready to serve.

2. To serve, spoon one-fourth of the sauce onto each dessert plate and top with the halved strawberries. Garnish with mint leaves.

The strawberries with wild blueberry sauce simply glow on their Purple Eve plate, and the colorful hydrangea-print tablecloth adds to this menu's tropical air.

White Veal Stew

Generally I would not dream of cooking up a stew in the summertime, but every now and then a rich, flavorful concoction like this, scented with nutmeg, fresh dill, and garlic, just seems perfect. I use only cubes of veal cut from the leg: it must be very young veal or it might be a bit tough after simmering for 45 minutes. The carrots can be julienned on a mandoline, as in the recipe, or cut into paper-thin ribbons with a vegetable peeler. The leeks are best julienned with a sharp chef's knife or cleaver.

I have been growing mâche successfully for several years. There are many types, and I find they all grow if planted in cool weather and picked before it becomes too hot. I like the variety *d'Étampes,* which has very dark green leaves, or *verte à coeur plein,* which has a full, round head. The radicchio I used is known as Treviso and is shaped like long thin leaves of cos lettuce. To grow radicchio, you must plant the seeds in the late summer for harvest the following spring or in the very early spring for harvest after the onset of cold weather.

My niece Sophie is extremely fond of frozen grapes, and she inspired this simple dessert. The red and green grapes are removed from their stems, frozen until hard, and then served in goblets with a small glass of Frangelico, a hazelnut liqueur. (Sophie is only four, so she eats her grapes with juice.)

This is an elegant summer menu and deserves a rather formal setting. I used an Arco China portion grill plate for the white veal stew, baked lemon rice, and steamed courgettes; the mâche and radicchio salad went on a Syracuse china plate; and the flatware is 1881 Rogers grape-pattern.

M E N U

BAKED LEMON RICE WITH HERBS
WHITE VEAL STEW
SALAD OF MÂCHE AND RADICCHIO
STEAMED COURGETTES
FROZEN GRAPES WITH FRANGELICO

Baked Lemon Rice with Herbs

SERVES 6

4 *tablespoons (½ stick) unsalted butter*
2 *shallots, peeled and finely minced*
2 *cups long-grain rice*
   Zest of 2 lemons
1 *sprig fresh tarragon*
3 *cups Chicken Stock (page 13)*
2 *tablespoons fresh tarragon leaves*
   Salt and freshly ground black pepper

1. Preheat the oven to 400° F.

2. Melt the butter in a medium flame-proof casserole and sauté the shallots until tender, 3 to 4 minutes. Add the rice and cook until translucent and well coated with butter, a few more minutes. Stir in half the lemon zest, the tarragon sprig, and the stock. Cover casserole, place in the oven, and bake until the liquid is absorbed and the rice tender, about 20 to 25 minutes.

3. Stir in the remaining lemon zest and the tarragon leaves; season to taste and serve immediately.

White Veal Stew

SERVES 6

6 tablespoons (¾ stick) unsalted butter
3 pounds boneless leg of veal, cut into 2-inch cubes
1 teaspoon salt
Freshly ground white pepper
1 clove garlic, peeled and finely minced
¾ cup finely chopped onions or shallots
3 tablespoons finely chopped fresh dill
¼ cup all-purpose flour
¼ teaspoon nutmeg, freshly grated
1 to 1¼ cups Chicken or Veal Stock (page 13)
1 cup water
2 carrots, peeled and finely julienned
2 leeks, trimmed, washed, and finely julienned
¾ cup heavy cream

1. In a large, flameproof casserole, melt 4 tablespoons of the butter. Add the veal and sprinkle with salt and pepper to taste. Cook over medium heat, stirring occasionally, until veal turns white, about 7 minutes. Add the garlic, onions or shallots, and 2 tablespoons of the dill; cook for 4 to 5 minutes.

2. Sprinkle on the flour and nutmeg. Add the stock and water and bring to a boil over high heat. Reduce the heat, cover, and simmer very slowly for 45 minutes, stirring once or twice. Do not let the liquid evaporate; add more stock if necessary.

3. In a large skillet, melt the remaining 2 tablespoons of butter. Add the carrots and leeks and toss in the butter until wilted, about 5 minutes. Add the wilted vegetables to the veal and stir in the cream. Heat until the stew comes to a simmer; sprinkle remaining tablespoon of dill on top right before serving.

Salad of Mâche and Radicchio

SERVES 6

1 handful of mâche and radicchio per person (we used Treviso radicchio)
3 tablespoons light olive oil
1 tablespoon fresh lemon juice
Salt and freshly ground black pepper

Arrange the mâche and radicchio on individual salad plates. Lightly dress with the oil and lemon juice, season to taste, and serve immediately.

Steamed Courgettes

SERVES 6

1 pound courgettes (baby zucchini)
4 tablespoons (½ stick) unsalted butter
Salt and freshly ground black pepper

1. Steam the courgettes over boiling water just until tender, 2 to 3 minutes. Remove from heat, let cool slightly, and cut into 1-inch diagonal slices.

2. In a large skillet, melt the butter. Toss the sliced courgettes to warm through, season to taste, then serve immediately.

Frozen Grapes with Frangelico

SERVES 6

Remove 1 pound red and 1 pound green seedless grapes from their stems. Place grapes on a tray lined with paper towels and freeze until hard. Serve in dessert dishes with a glass of Frangelico (hazelnut liqueur), or with a little Frangelico sprinkled on the grapes.

Parchment Bluefish

Being a Quick Cook means being organized, buying and stocking the right foods, and—very important—having the right equipment and supplies. Parchment paper, for example, is an essential item. An opaque, strong, uncoated paper, it is available in large sheets from baking supply stores (boxes of 1,000 pieces are reasonably priced) or on rolls in kitchenware and gourmet stores. I use it to line baking sheets (eliminating the need for buttering or greasing), to line baking trays or roasting pans (drips remain on the parchment so you don't have to scrub the tray), and to wrap pork and veal when roasting (it keeps the meat succulent). When I poach fish or fruits I often cover them with parchment to retain their moisture, and when making candies or praline I line my marble slab with parchment instead of butter or oil.

Parchment can also be used to cook *en papillote* red snapper fillets, black bass, and fillet of sole; even breast of chicken can be wrapped up with a mélange of tender vegetables and herbs. In this menu, the fillets of bluefish are flavored with slices of lemon, oregano, and parsley and wrapped in a semicircle of parchment. The edges are crimped closed; in the hot oven, the airtight package puffs up and the fish cooks in its own steam. You can serve the package right on the plate (insert a sharp knife to release the steam), or you can unwrap the meat or fish before serving—as we did here.

Pastina is the baby food of pastas—tiny, star-shaped forms of delicate egg pasta that cook in a few minutes. I like to serve pastina with herb flavorings, in this case finely chopped chives. The chopped salad with its creamy avocado dressing adds a wonderfully colorful element to the table.

The crème brûlée with fresh blueberries is served in a large scallop shell (the kind used for coquilles St. Jacques). Remember that with crème brûlée it is very important to caramelize the sugar under a hot broiler so that the creamy dessert has a lovely, crunchy topping.

Sometimes when I cook en papillote I bring the food to the table in its parchment package, but if there are other items on the plate—like the pastina with chives that accompanies this parchment bluefish—I remove the paper first for a neater presentation. The periwinkle and yellow Harlequin plates provide a contrast to the pale shades of the fish and pasta; the glass is early American, clover pattern.

M E N U

PARCHMENT BLUEFISH
PASTINA WITH CHIVES
CHOPPED SALAD WITH CREAMY AVOCADO DRESSING
CRÈME BRÛLÉE WITH BLUEBERRIES

Parchment Bluefish

SERVES 2

2 tablespoons olive oil
1 small shallot, peeled and finely
  minced
1 sprig fresh oregano
2 fresh bluefish fillets, approximately
  ⅓ pound each
2 teaspoons unsalted butter
4 sprigs fresh flat Italian parsley
1 lemon, thinly sliced

1. Preheat the oven to 450° F. Cut 2 rounds of parchment paper 14 to 16 inches in diameter. Fold each in half.

2. In a small skillet, heat the olive oil and gently sauté the shallot and oregano just until softened, 5 minutes.

3. Place 1 fillet on each parchment round. Spoon half the sautéed mixture over each fish, dot with butter, and top with sprigs of parsley and slices of lemon. Fold the parchment over and seal the edges by crimping them.

4. Bake until the parchment has puffed, 10 to 13 minutes. Remove the fish from the parchment and serve immediately.

Pastina with Chives

SERVES 2

½ cup pastina (very small pasta beads)
1 tablespoon unsalted butter
1 tablespoon chopped fresh chives
  Salt to taste

1. Cook the pastina in a saucepan of boiling water according to package directions. Drain well.

2. Melt the butter in a medium skillet and add the chives. Stir in the pastina, warm thoroughly, add salt, and serve.

Chopped Salad with Creamy Avocado Dressing

SERVES 2 GENEROUSLY

Creamy Avocado Dressing
MAKES ½ CUP

1 ripe avocado (we prefer the dark-
  skinned Haas variety)
¼ teaspoon fresh lemon juice
½ cup Mayonnaise (page 11)
1 tablespoon chopped fresh chives
1 small shallot, peeled and finely
  minced
  Salt and freshly ground black pepper

1 handful coarsely chopped radicchio
1 handful coarsely chopped chicory
½ red bell pepper, seeded and coarsely
  chopped
½ yellow bell pepper, seeded and
  coarsely chopped
½ green bell pepper, seeded and
  coarsely chopped
2 radishes, trimmed and thinly sliced
½ cup crunchy bean sprouts
1 hard-boiled egg, shell removed and
  egg finely chopped

1. To make the dressing, mash the avocado with the lemon juice. Place with the mayonnaise in the jar of a blender or a food processor and blend until smooth. Stir in the chives and shallot, season to taste, and refrigerate until ready to serve. (If the dressing will not be used for a while, place the avocado pit in the dressing to prevent mixture from turning brown.)

2. Combine all ingredients for salad except the egg in a large bowl and toss.

3. To serve, place a generous handful of the chopped salad ingredients on individual plates and spoon the dressing over. Top each with some of the chopped egg.

Crème Brûlée with Blueberries

SERVES 4

1 cup heavy cream
½ vanilla bean, split lengthwise
2 egg yolks, lightly beaten and strained
¼ cup sugar
¾ tablespoon unsalted butter, chilled
and cut into small pieces
1 cup fresh blueberries

1. Place the cream and vanilla bean in a heavy saucepan and bring to a boil. Reduce heat and simmer for 5 minutes, stirring occasionally. Set aside.

2. Whisk egg yolks and 2 tablespoons sugar in the top of a double boiler over simmering water until pale, thick, and fluffy. Do not overcook or mixture will scramble.

3. Remove the vanilla bean from the cream. Strain the cream into the egg-sugar mixture, whisking constantly. Cook slowly, stirring occasionally, until mixture thickens and coats the back of a spoon, 10 minutes.

4. Remove from the heat and whisk in the butter.

5. Divide the blueberries among 4 large (6-inch) shallow scallop shells or small porcelain gratin dishes. Pour the custard mixture over the berries and chill thoroughly.

6. Preheat the broiler.

7. Immediately before serving, sprinkle the remaining 2 tablespoons sugar over the crème brûlée and place each dish under the broiler to caramelize the sugar, taking care not to burn it.

The last step in making crème brûlée is to caramelize the sugar topping under a broiler, so this dessert must be made in dishes that will withstand very high heat. I often use scallop shells— the same ones I use for making coquilles St. Jacques; they won't crack, and they look so pretty.

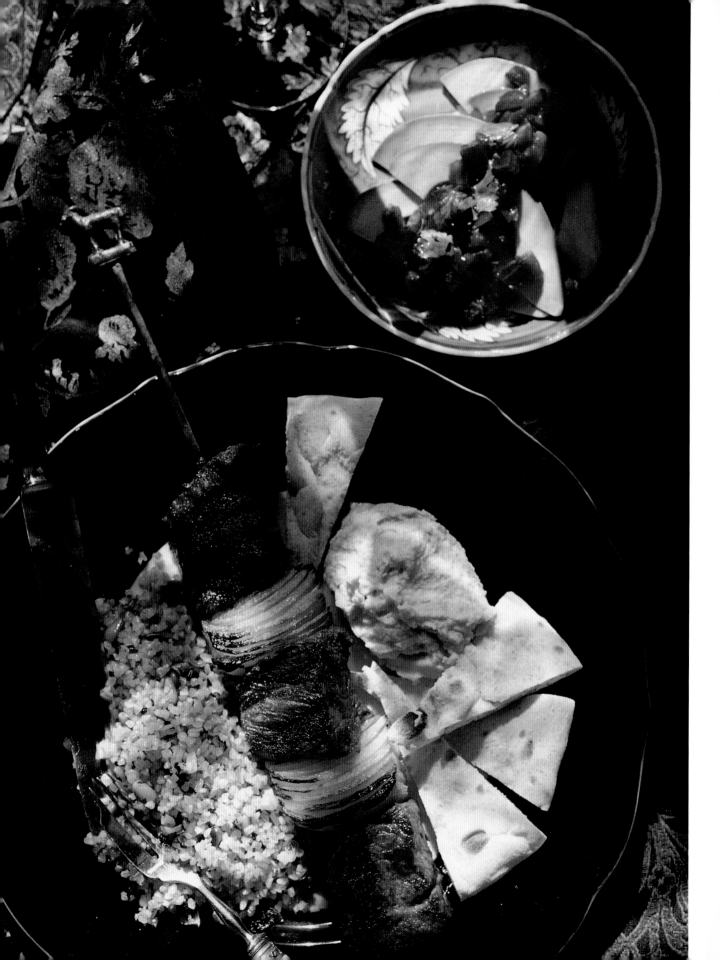

Beef and Red Onion Kabobs

On my second date with Andy, he took me to New York's Balkan Armenian Restaurant. I remember ordering shish kabobs of beef and lamb flavored with cumin or turmeric, lemon, garlic, and olive oil, then grilled over an open fire. I decided then and there that I had to visit the region that produced such food—and three years later we made a trip to Greece, Yugoslavia, and Turkey, where I learned how to make this wonderful kabob dish.

For this menu we threaded 2-inch beef cubes with fresh red onion onto decorative metal skewers. It is important to use the right cut of meat: we used a "beef triangle," which is cut from right under the sirloin. Because it has no fat or gristle but is well marbled, it is perfect for cubing and grilling. The marinade is very important, too, in flavoring and tenderizing the meat.

The kabobs are served with slices of ripe, unbruised avocado fanned on individual plates and topped with a chunky tomato-coriander dressing. The hummus, made from chick peas, garlic, lemon juice, and olive oil, is eaten with wedges of toasted pita bread or Armenian flat bread, which you can find in the gourmet section of many groceries. The bulgur pilaf is another staple of Eastern Mediterranean and Middle Eastern cooking and is very easy to make.

I call this method of serving melon "carpaccio," because the delicate strips remind me of the papery raw beef in the classic Italian carpaccio dish. Topped with a scoop of fruit ice, this makes for an unusually attractive presentation.

Like me, my assistant Amanda collects odd china from diners: the black plate under this beef and red onion kabob is a very unusual example from her stock. It was amusing to mix it with early English porcelain, Bakelite-handled knives, and tortoise-handled forks.

M E N U

TOMATO-CORIANDER AVOCADOS
BEEF AND RED ONION KABOBS
BULGUR PILAF WITH PINE NUTS
MELON WITH RASPBERRY GRANITÉ

Tomato-Coriander Avocados

SERVES 4

2 *ripe, unbruised avocados*

Tomato-Coriander Dressing
MAKES APPROXIMATELY ½ CUP
4 *ripe plum tomatoes, seeded and cut into ¼-inch squares*
1 *teaspoon red wine vinegar*
1 *tablespoon olive oil*
1 *tablespoon chopped fresh coriander (cilantro)*
Juice of ¼ lime
Salt and freshly ground black pepper

1. Carefully remove the skin and pits of the avocados. Slice each lengthwise into thin strips. Allowing half an avocado per person, fan the slices onto individual salad plates.

2. Whisk all dressing ingredients together and spoon over avocado fans.

Beef and Red Onion Kabobs

2 pounds boneless beef, cut into 2-inch cubes
5 tablespoons olive oil
1 tablespoon ground cumin
2 medium red onions, cut into eighths

Hummus
1 (19-ounce) can chick peas, drained
1 large clove garlic, peeled and sliced
Juice of 1 lemon
⅓ cup olive oil
Salt to taste

1. Place the cubes of beef in a large bowl and toss with 4 tablespoons of olive oil. Sprinkle the cumin over the beef and mix to coat the cubes thoroughly. Let marinate at room temperature for 30 minutes or overnight in the refrigerator.

2. Remove the meat from the marinade and thread the cubes onto long metal skewers, alternating meat cubes with wedges of onion. (You should have 4 to 6 skewers.)

3. Brush the kabobs lightly with the remaining tablespoon of oil and grill over hot coals, turning occasionally, until they are nicely browned, about 10 to 20 minutes.

4. To make the hummus, combine all ingredients in a food processor and process until smooth. Serve at room temperature with the kabobs.

Bulgur Pilaf with Pine Nuts

1 cup bulgur (cracked wheat)
2 tablespoons olive oil
2 tablespoons pine nuts (pignoli), toasted
1 small onion, peeled and finely chopped
2 tablespoons finely chopped fresh mint
Salt and freshly ground black pepper

1. Put the bulgur in a bowl, cover with water, and let soak for 45 minutes.

2. Drain the bulgur through a sieve, shaking it gently to remove as much water as possible.

3. Heat 1 tablespoon of olive oil in a large skillet. Add the pine nuts and sauté over low heat until lightly browned, approximately 2 minutes. Remove the pine nuts from the skillet.

4. Add the remaining oil to the skillet and sauté the onion until tender, 3 to 5 minutes. Add the drained bulgur to the skillet and sauté for 5 minutes. Stir in the pine nuts and mint, season to taste, heat through, and serve.

Melon with Raspberry Granité

½ ripe orange-fleshed honeydew melon, seeded
½ ripe green honeydew melon, seeded

Raspberry Granité
MAKES APPROXIMATELY 1 PINT
2 cups frozen, unsweetened red raspberries, thawed
1 cup water
¾ cup sugar

1. Cut each melon into eighths and remove skin with a sharp knife. With a sharp vegetable peeler slice melon into paper-thin ribbons. Cover and chill until ready to use.

2. To make the granité, place the raspberries and their juice in a sieve over a medium bowl and mash them with a wooden spoon, extracting as much pulp and juice as possible without forcing any seeds through. Set aside.

3. Combine the water and sugar in a small saucepan over medium heat and cook until the sugar dissolves; continue to cook the mixture approximately 3 to 4 minutes longer.

4. Add the sugar syrup to the raspberry puree and chill thoroughly.

5. Freeze the raspberry mixture in an ice-cream maker according to the manufacturer's directions.

6. Divide and arrange the melon "carpaccio" on individual dessert plates and place a scoop or two of raspberry granité on top. Serve immediately.

This melon "carpaccio" with its scoop of homemade raspberry granité is one of the most beautiful desserts I have ever seen; sitting on its green and white diner plate, it looks like a particularly exotic flower.

Steamed Fillet of Salmon

Most people, I suppose, would find my kitchen well equipped, but I have a friend whose kitchen far surpasses mine. Her shelves are filled with such items as 24 footed porcelain bowls for soupe à l'oignon, 16 dishes for eggs brouillé, and 36 silver egg cups. She also has 12 Chinese bamboo steamers that she often uses for a steamer meal.

We are so accustomed to sautéing or frying or poaching or broiling that we have overlooked steaming as a quick and nutritious method of cooking meat and fish. The main course for this menu is a perfect example of steamer cooking: by placing the fish atop a mixture of fresh herbs, little salt or spice is necessary. Indeed, you could eat the salmon plain, but I like to serve it with a cream-sorrel sauce, or with homemade mayonnaise or a red pepper sauce.

The three-pea salad is especially good in early summer when all types of peas are readily available. (Frozen baby peas—petit pois—can be substituted for fresh, but I do not use frozen snow or sugar snap peas.)

If one has a supply of tart shells in the freezer, fruit tarts are perfectly possible for a Quick Cook meal. We used Friar plums for these tarts, but Santa Rosa, greengage, or elephant heart plums would be good substitutes.

M E N U
STEAMED FILLET OF SALMON
ORZO WITH WILD MUSHROOMS
THREE-PEA MÉLANGE WITH ORANGE ZEST
FRESH GARDEN SALAD
PLUM TARTLETS

A Chinese bamboo steamer with several racks can be used to cook a whole meal or just one element, like this fillet of salmon.

Preceding page: *This meal of steamed salmon with cream-sorrel sauce, orzo with mushrooms, and a three-pea mélange had such lovely, delicate colors I took special care to design a soft yet summery table setting: the dinner plates are by Simlay, the glasses are Depression amber, and we rolled the yellow linen napkins into old simulated-ivory rings.*

Steamed Fillet of Salmon

SERVES 6

Cream-Sorrel Sauce
  1 tablespoon unsalted butter
  1 bunch fresh sorrel leaves, cut into a chiffonnade (fine shreds)
  ¼ cup heavy cream
     Salt and freshly ground black pepper

  6 (⅓ pound) fresh salmon fillets
     Several small bunches of fresh herbs (chervil, basil, mint, tarragon)

1. To make the sauce, melt the butter in a medium skillet. Add the sorrel leaves and sauté until limp, about 2 minutes. Stir in the cream, season to taste, and heat through. Keep the sauce warm while preparing the fish.

2. Line each tier of a multilayered Chinese bamboo steamer with the herbs and arrange single layers of the salmon pieces on top of the herbs. Place additional herbs on top of the salmon.

3. Place the steamer in a large skillet and add 2 inches of boiling water. Cover and steam the fish until done, 7 to 10 minutes.

4. Remove the salmon fillets, garnish

with a fresh herb sprig, and serve warm with the sauce.

NOTE: Do not stack more than 3 tiers of the bamboo steamer or the fish will not cook properly. If you need more, use another steamer and skillet.

Orzo with Wild Mushrooms

SERVES 6

  2 cups orzo (rice-shaped pasta)
  4 tablespoons (½ stick) unsalted butter
  ½ pound shiitake mushrooms, finely cut crosswise
  ⅓ cup fresh chives, cut into 1-inch lengths
     Salt and freshly ground black pepper
     Freshly grated Parmesan cheese (optional)

1. Cook the orzo according to package directions until just tender. Drain well and keep warm.

2. In a large skillet, melt the butter and sauté the mushrooms until tender, approximately 3 minutes.

3. Add the orzo and chives to the mushrooms; season to taste. Sprinkle with Parmesan cheese, if desired, and serve hot.

Three-Pea Mélange with Orange Zest

SERVES 6

  ⅓ pound snow peas, strings removed
  ⅓ pound sugar-snap peas, stem ends and strings removed
  ¾ cup shelled baby peas
  2 tablespoons (¼ stick) unsalted butter
     Zest of ¼ orange
     Pinch of sugar
     Salt to taste

1. In a large pot of boiling water, blanch each variety of pea separately just until tender, no longer than 3 to 4 minutes. Plunge peas in ice water to stop the cooking and drain well.

2. Melt the butter in a large skillet and add the drained peas. Sauté until heated through. Add the orange zest, sugar, and salt and gently toss. Serve hot.

Fresh Garden Salad

SERVES 4

1 large handful of salad greens per person (I like to use bibb, oakleaf, and ruby lettuce in summer)

Dressing
MAKES ¼ CUP

 2 tablespoons hazelnut oil
¼ cup safflower oil
¼ cup olive oil
 1 tablespoon fresh lemon juice
 1 tablespoon Dijon mustard
 2 tablespoons heavy cream
¼ cup chopped fresh coriander (cilantro)
 Salt and freshly ground black pepper

Place salad greens in serving bowl. Whisk dressing ingredients together and toss with salad greens right before serving.

Plum Tartlets

SERVES 4

Approximately 12 ripe, dark red plums, preferably Friar
6 *prebaked 4½-inch Tart Shells (page 11)*
2 *tablespoons sugar*
 Freshly grated nutmeg to taste

 1 *tablespoon unsalted butter, at room temperature*
½ *cup heavy cream*
 1 *tablespoon sugar*
 1 *tablespoon dark rum*

1. Preheat oven to 350° F.

2. Halve the plums and remove the pits. Arrange as many halves as possible, cut side down, in the tart shells. Cut the remaining plums into ¼-inch slices and arrange them between the plum halves. Sprinkle with sugar and nutmeg and dot with butter.

3. Bake the tartlets until the fruit is tender and the crust nicely browned, 20 to 25 minutes. Let cool.

4. Whip cream together with sugar and rum. Chill until ready to serve.

An old-fashioned setting for an old-fashioned dessert— the individual plum tartlets fit snugly into antique Wedgewood yellowware plates; the flatware is old Rogers fiddle-pattern.

Green Enchiladas

In Texas and elsewhere in the South, hostesses never seem afraid to serve local fare—people are proud of their regional cuisine. I've been served superb Southern cooking in Jackson, Mississippi; Creole and Cajun feasts in New Orleans; and an extraordinary soul-food dinner in Amarillo, Texas. At one Dallas party we were served Texas barbecue on Meissen china with huge, white damask napkins. That was too much for me—I just couldn't wipe the sauce off my fingers on that beautiful cloth, so I asked the butler for paper napkins. I do think the hostess was relieved, for she took paper napkins also.

It was in Texas, too, that I was served this terrific Mexican food at a friend's dinner party. Beginning the meal with piña coladas, we consumed large quantities of fresh tortilla chips with a great salsa called Pico de Gallo. We were then served a wonderful casserole of green enchiladas—flour tortillas wrapped around a mixture of chicken and spinach. The salad combined avocados, jicama, red onions, and oranges dressed with lime juice, vinegar, and oil—a refreshing, unique, and flavorful combination.

Dessert was the traditional Spanish or Mexican flan, or caramel cup custard. And our hostess remembered another traditional accompaniment: wedges of red, ripe watermelon sprinkled with coarse salt were served alongside the entire meal.

I baked these enchiladas in the bottom half of my Moroccan tagine— an excellent, all-purpose "casserole" dish—and then served this traditional Mexican meal on old, hand-painted Mexican pottery that I bought from a collector. Note the salt-sprinkled watermelon wedges that accompany the tortilla chips and pico de gallo.

M E N U

PIÑA COLADAS
TORTILLA CHIPS WITH PICO DE GALLO
GREEN ENCHILADAS
MEXICAN SALAD
FLAN CUPS

Piña Coladas

MAKES 1 GENEROUS OR 2 MEDIUM DRINKS

Ice cubes
1 cup unsweetened pineapple juice
¼ cup cream of coconut
⅓ cup light rum (optional)

1. Fill a blender jar halfway with small ice cubes or crushed ice.

2. Add the remaining ingredients to the blender and blend until light and frothy. Serve immediately.

Tortilla Chips with Pico de Gallo

SERVES 6

12 fresh corn tortillas
   Corn or light vegetable oil
 1 clove garlic, peeled and crushed
   Salt to taste

Pico de Gallo Sauce
MAKES 2 TO 3 CUPS
 4 large ripe tomatoes, chopped
 ½ cup finely chopped scallions
 3 fresh jalapeño peppers, seeded and finely minced
 1 clove garlic, peeled and finely minced
 ¼ cup fresh lime juice
 ½ cup chopped fresh coriander (cilantro)
 1 teaspoon finely chopped fresh oregano
   Salt and freshly ground black pepper

1. To make the chips, cut the tortillas into sixths and fry the wedges in medium-hot (375° F.) oil until crisp. Drain well on paper towels and place in a brown paper bag. Shake with crushed garlic clove and salt.

2. To make the sauce, combine all ingredients and refrigerate, covered, until serving time. (This sauce is best made 1 to 2 hours before using.) Serve with warm or room-temperature tortilla chips.

Green Enchiladas

SERVES 6

 2 pounds boneless chicken breasts
 4 tablespoons (½ stick) unsalted butter
 1 large white onion, peeled and finely chopped
 1 pound fresh spinach, well washed
 3 cups sour cream
 2 (4-ounce) cans green chiles, drained and chopped
 1 teaspoon ground cumin
 ¼ cup milk
   Salt to taste
12 flour tortillas
 6 ounces Monterey Jack cheese, grated

1. Poach the chicken breasts in a small skillet or saucepan with water to cover until done, 15 to 20 minutes. Remove from water, cool slightly, and shred into small, bite-size pieces. Set aside.

2. In a small skillet, melt the butter and sauté the onion until tender, about 5 minutes.

3. Preheat oven to 350° F. Lightly butter a large casserole.

4. Steam the spinach in a steamer or colander. Drain, reserving ½ cup of the cooking liquid. Let the spinach cool slightly; chop coarsely.

5. Combine the onion, spinach, sour cream, chiles, cumin, reserved spinach liquid, and milk; mix well and season to taste.

6. Add half the sauce to the shredded chicken and mix well. Place the tortillas in the oven to soften (about 3 minutes) and remove. Fill the tortillas with equal amounts of filling and roll up. Place the rolled tortillas seam side down in 1 layer in the prepared casserole. Cover with half the grated cheese and top with the remaining sauce; sprinkle on the remaining cheese. Bake until heated through, about 30 minutes.

Mexican Salad

SERVES 6

3 oranges, peeled and sectioned

1 large red onion, peeled, halved, and thinly sliced lengthwise

3 ripe avocados, peeled, pitted, and cut into lengthwise wedges

1 jicama, peeled and cut into thin strips

Dressing

Juice of 1 lime

⅛ cup white wine vinegar

¼ cup light vegetable oil

Salt and freshly ground black pepper

Arrange orange sections, onion slices, avocado wedges, and jicama strips on a platter. Mix dressing ingredients in a bowl and drizzle over the salad right before serving.

Flan Cups

SERVES 6

1¼ cups sugar

¼ cup water

2 cups milk or half-and-half

½ vanilla bean, split lengthwise

3 eggs, lightly beaten

1. Preheat the oven to 350° F.

2. In a very heavy saucepan, melt 1 cup sugar with water over low heat until it becomes clear. (Swirl the mixture; do not stir or the syrup will cloud.) Raise the heat and cook until the syrup turns a light golden color. Pour a small amount of syrup into each of 6 custard cups or individual soufflé dishes (approximately ½-cup capacity) and spread it evenly on the bottom. The syrup will harden as it cools.

3. In a medium saucepan, scald the milk or half-and-half with the vanilla bean and remaining ¼ cup sugar.

4. Place the beaten eggs in a bowl and gradually pour the hot milk mixture over them in a slow, steady stream, whisking vigorously. Strain mixture into the prepared cups, discarding vanilla bean.

5. Place the custard cups in a large roasting pan or baking dish and add enough boiling water to reach halfway up the sides of the cups. Bake until the custards are set, 30 to 45 minutes.

6. Chill the custards well. To serve, invert the custards onto serving plates.

Summer Frittata

W e used to spend a great deal of time in the Tuscany region of Italy, in a little town called Camaiore, where a good friend of Andy's had a lovely villa. It's an area famous for its white marble: Michelangelo used a nearby quarry, and at the time we used to visit, Jacques Lipchitz and Henry Moore both maintained studios there.

Tuscany is also famous for its food, particularly simple country fare making much use of local herbs and of olive oil (especially oil from Lucca, in northern Tuscany). The tomato soup in this menu is a typical dish: a simple concoction of plum tomatoes simmered with a mirepoix of three or four other vegetables and flavored with basil.

We were often entertained, and at almost every party we were served some type of frittata or omelet. The frittata was baked in a hot oven with lots of olive oil or cooked in a flat sauté pan on top of the stove and turned once to finish the cooking. These omelets were filled with amazing things, including fresh baby peas, various local cheeses, greens, or wild mushrooms. The frittata recipe in this menu is a stovetop edition with two different toppings or fillings.

The white bean salad comes from a recipe that I learned in Florence. You can use canned or fresh cannellini beans; if dried beans are substituted, they often split during preparation, and the salad is not so pretty. A simple dressing of garlic, olive oil, scallions, and red onion is sufficient to enhance the beans.

The dessert is merely fresh, halved, very ripe strawberries and ripe red raspberries. The touch of flavor added by the zest of lemon and orange is sufficient if the fruit is really fresh and ripe.

These neoclassic-pattern ironstone portion plates are really a very fancy restaurantware made by Booths of England; with cobalt-blue Depression glass and pearl-handled silver, they are the perfect setting for a summer frittata lunch.

M E N U

TOMATO SOUP
SUMMER FRITTATA
WHITE BEAN SALAD
ZESTED SUMMER BERRIES

This fresh-tasting tomato soup was served in a plain white bowl atop a McNichol china plate; the linen cloth and napkins are woven in a simple blue and yellow plaid.

Tomato Soup

SERVES 4

4   tablespoons (½ stick) unsalted butter
½   cup thinly sliced celery
½   cup thinly sliced leek
¼   cup thinly sliced shallots

3   cups canned plum tomatoes with juice
3   whole fresh basil leaves
    Salt and freshly ground black pepper
    Torn fresh basil leaves, for garnish

1. In a large saucepan, melt the butter and sauté the celery, leek, and shallots until softened, about 5 minutes.

2. Add the tomatoes to the pan, crushing them a bit with a wooden spoon. Stir in the basil leaves and simmer for 15 minutes.

3. Season the soup to taste and garnish with basil leaves before serving.

Summer Frittata

SERVES 4

½   cup olive oil
9   eggs, lightly beaten
    Salt and freshly ground black pepper

Topping 1
4   cloves garlic, peeled and minced
1   small bunch broccoli rabe, coarsely chopped
½   cup fresh porcini mushrooms, cleaned and thinly sliced

Topping 2
3   scallions, trimmed and thinly sliced
6   yellow cherry tomatoes, thinly sliced
10 to 12 fresh sage leaves

1. Heat all but about 3 tablespoons of the olive oil in a heavy 10-inch skillet. Pour the eggs into the hot pan and cook over medium-low heat for 4 to 6 minutes, drawing the eggs away from the sides of the pan with a fork or small spatula so that the uncooked eggs run to the sides and cook.

2. Spread topping of your choice on the eggs and cook 2 to 4 minutes longer.

3. Heat the remaining oil in a 12-inch skillet. Carefully loosen the frittata from its smaller pan and flip it into the larger one, top side down. Cook 3 to 4 minutes, making sure the eggs are cooked through. Carefully invert the frittata onto a warm platter, season with salt and pepper, and serve immediately.

White Bean Salad

SERVES 4

2 (15-ounce) cans cannellini beans, rinsed and drained
½ cup finely chopped red onions
8 cloves garlic, roasted, peeled, and left whole (see Note)
3 scallions, cut into 2- to 3-inch thin slivers
2 tablespoons olive oil
Salt and freshly ground black pepper

1. Combine the beans, onions, garlic, and scallions in a large bowl.

2. Drizzle the olive oil over the mixture and season to taste. Serve cool or at room temperature.

NOTE: To roast the garlic, place the whole unpeeled head in a preheated 350° F. oven. Bake until soft and browned, about 1 hour.

Zested Summer Berries

SERVES 4

2 pints ripe strawberries, hulled and cut in half
1 cup ripe red raspberries
Zest of 1 lemon
Zest of ½ orange

Gently combine the strawberries and raspberries with the citrus zests. Arrange on a platter.

Strawberries look even more beautiful when they are hulled and cut in half lengthwise; I think they also taste better this way. The lemon and orange peel was removed with a zester.

Rack of Lamb

Here in Westport there is a terrific store called Hay Day that carries a fine line of meats that come vacuum packed. My favorite is the baby rack of lamb: eight tiny rib chops with "Frenched" bones (trimmed of all meat and fat) and ready to cook. I have taken to marinating them for at least 30 minutes, then grilling them. They can also be put under the broiler, but the flavor is very good when they are cooked over a hickory or fruitwood charcoal fire. These racks are so tender and so small that they take only about 10 minutes to grill if the coals are extremely hot, and you must be very careful not to char the bones or the meat.

With the lamb I serve a very simple salad of red plum and yellow cherry tomatoes with cubed feta cheese and a balsamic vinegar dressing. Cherry tomatoes now come in many sizes, shapes, and colors; look for variety to make a salad special. The summer salad is just mâche with tarragon dressing, and the baby peas are cooked with a chiffonade of lettuce.

There are new varieties of melon on the market these days: don't hesitate to try the chanterais, the Hand melon, the juicy muskmelon, and the orange-fleshed honeydew. But then don't forget the honeydew or cantaloupe—with a bit of fresh mint to enhance the flavor, these plain melons are simply wonderful.

M E N U

RACK OF LAMB
TOMATOES WITH FETA CHEESE
BABY PEAS AND ESCAROLE
SUMMER SALAD
MINTED MELON BALLS

The baby lamb sits with the marinade flavoring for at least 30 minutes; the actual grilling takes only about 10 minutes, depending on the size of the rack. Note how the lamb is trimmed French-style, with the rib bones left long.

Preceding page: Rack of lamb is traditionally a very formal dish, and it is fun to serve it in an informal setting. I decorated this picnic table with a striped, crocheted runner and set it with tan enamelware dinner plates and my old green Bakelite-handled flatware.

Opposite: I served the minted melon balls in cheerful, striped Depression glass plates and tucked a few chocolate decorated cookies alongside.

Rack of Lamb

SERVES 4

1 baby rack of lamb with at least 8 chops, well trimmed and with rib bones left long
1 tablespoon balsamic vinegar
2 tablespoons olive oil
3 to 4 sprigs fresh thyme

1. With a sharp knife, cut a diagonal crisscross pattern in the outside layer of fat on the rack. Rub the lamb with the vinegar and oil and place the thyme on top. Let sit for 30 minutes, while you prepare the grill.

2. Grill the rack over very hot coals for 5 minutes on each side, or slightly longer if desired. The meat should be pink, 160°–165° F on a meat thermometer. Slice into individual chops and serve hot.

Tomatoes with Feta Cheese

SERVES 4

3 ripe red plum tomatoes, cut into ¼ slices
1 pint yellow cherry tomatoes, halved
¼ pound feta cheese, cut into ½-inch cubes
1 tablespoon balsamic vinegar
Salt and freshly ground black pepper

Place the tomatoes in a serving bowl and toss gently with the vinegar. Season to taste and arrange the cheese on top. Serve immediately.

Baby Peas and Escarole

SERVES 4

2 cups shelled baby peas (1½ pounds unshelled), or frozen petit pois

1 tablespoon unsalted butter
2 small heads escarole, cut into chiffonnade (fine shreds)
1 teaspoon sugar
Salt and freshly ground black pepper

1. Cook the peas in a small amount of boiling water until just tender, 4 to 5 minutes. Drain well.

2. Melt the butter in a small skillet and soften the escarole strips over low heat, 1 to 2 minutes. Sprinkle with sugar and season to taste. Add the peas to the lettuce and toss gently. Serve immediately.

Summer Salad

SERVES 4

1 handful of mâche (lamb's lettuce) per person, torn into pieces
1 tablespoon tarragon vinegar
¼ cup light olive oil
Salt and freshly ground black pepper

Toss the mâche with the vinegar and oil and season to taste. Serve immediately.

Minted Melon Balls

SERVES 4

1 ripe cantaloupe
½ small, ripe honeydew
1 bunch fresh mint

1. Halve the cantaloupe and seed both melons. With a melon-ball scoop, make as many balls as possible, trying to keep them whole and the same size. Place the melon balls in a bowl.

2. Tear the mint leaves into small pieces and sprinkle over the melon. Stir gently and chill for at least 30 minutes.

3. Serve the melon balls on individual dessert plates with a favorite cookie.

Grilled Tuna with Orange Butter

This very simple meal of grilled tuna was served out on the open porch, and I set a very informal table. The cutout printed cotton runner was most likely a dresser scarf; the dinner plates are pale blue T.S. & T. Lu-Ray Pastels, made in America; and the beer was served in old-fashioned jelly jars. The copper dove is one of a pair of Victorian garden ornaments.

The mind's ability to catalogue a taste is great, I find. When I try to remember where I first ate this or that—in which restaurant, in which country, in what year—I can usually pinpoint the exact spot. Consider the stuffed yellow peppers in this menu. I had something very similar in a tiny restaurant in Florence when I was traveling there with Andy in 1963; I remember being amazed at the array of cooked, stuffed vegetables displayed on homespun cloths in that charming restaurant on a small street not far from the Boboli Gardens. (If I studied a map, I could most likely find the street—even twenty-five years later.)

These peppers are stuffed with a mixture of rice, onions, currants, dry and fresh coriander, basil, and parsley. Olive oil is used generously. The peppers are baked covered until tender and then uncovered until slightly browned. The same rice filling can be used for tomatoes, zucchini, eggplants, and summer squash. (If you're stuffing an eggplant, I suggest roasting it first in a hot oven for 20 or 30 minutes, then cutting it in half lengthwise and scooping out the center flesh to make room for the stuffing.) The filling can also be varied by adding cooked ground meat, the chopped flesh of the vegetable, other herbs, and so on.

Tuna has become increasingly available, and it is one of the nicest fishes to grill. A fresh tuna steak, cut ¾ to 1 inch thick, should weigh about ⅓ to ½ pound—a generous portion for one, especially if you're serving the rest of this menu. The orange butter, subtly flavored with chopped savory or parsley, complements the delicate taste of the fish wonderfully.

The sliced tomatoes with the tarragon-cream topping are also wonderful, and so easy. If the tomatoes have thickish skins, pull them off with a sharp knife; otherwise just slice them, arrange them on a platter, and spoon the cream on top. The peach crumble is another homey and desirable dessert that everyone seems to crave, and there will be no leftovers—guaranteed!

M E N U
GRILLED TUNA WITH ORANGE BUTTER
SLICED TOMATOES WITH TARRAGON CREAM
BAKED STUFFED YELLOW PEPPERS
PEACH CRUMBLE

Grilled Tuna with Orange Butter

SERVES 4

6 tablespoons (¾ stick) unsalted
  butter, at room temperature
  Zest and juice of 1 orange
1 tablespoon chopped fresh summer
  savory or parsley
1½ pounds fresh tuna, cut into ¾-inch-
  thick steaks
  Salt and freshly ground black pepper
  Orange wedges

1. In a small bowl, beat the softened butter with the orange zest. Beating constantly, slowly add the orange juice. Stir in the savory or parsley and set aside.

2. Place the tuna on a grill over hot coals. (Be sure to spray grill with vegetable oil to prevent sticking.) Grill 4 minutes on each side or to desired degree of doneness, brushing with some of the orange butter while grilling.

3. Remove the steaks from the grill and season to taste. Serve hot with remaining orange butter and the wedges.

NOTE: When buying fresh tuna, choose fish that is deep red in color and free of any dark spots.

Sliced Tomatoes with Tarragon Cream

SERVES 4

4 large, ripe beefsteak tomatoes, cut
  into ¼-inch slices
¼ cup Crème Fraîche (page 11)
¼ cup heavy cream
¼ teaspoon coarse salt
1 tablespoon fresh tarragon leaves
  Fresh tarragon leaves, for garnish

Arrange the tomato slices in an overlapping pattern on a shallow dish or platter. In a medium bowl, mix the crème fraîche, heavy cream, salt, and tarragon. Spoon this mixture over the sliced tomatoes and garnish with tarragon leaves. Serve immediately.

Baked Stuffed Yellow Peppers

SERVES 4

1½ cups water
¼ teaspoon salt
¾ cup long-grain white rice
⅓ cup olive oil
1 large onion, peeled and very thinly
  sliced
2 cloves garlic, peeled and finely
  chopped
1 teaspoon ground coriander
1 tablespoon chopped fresh coriander
  (cilantro)
1 tablespoon chopped fresh basil, or
  1 teaspoon dried
1 tablespoon chopped fresh flat Italian
  parsley
3 tablespoons dried currants soaked in
  ¼ cup orange juice
1 tablespoon chopped sun-dried
  tomatoes
  Salt and freshly ground black pepper
4 large yellow bell peppers

1. Preheat oven to 350° F.

2. In a medium saucepan, bring water and salt to a boil. Add the rice, reduce heat, and cook, covered, until almost tender, 12 to 15 minutes. Set aside.

3. In a large skillet, heat 3 tablespoons of the olive oil over moderate heat. Add the onion and garlic and cook 10 minutes, stirring occasionally. Stir in rice, coriander, herbs, drained currants, sundried tomatoes, and salt and pepper to taste.

4. With a sharp knife, carefully cut out

the stem tops from the peppers. Remove the seeds and membranes inside. Set tops aside. Arrange the peppers in a deep, covered casserole rubbed with olive oil so they fit snugly and fill each with an equal amount of the rice mixture. Drizzle the remaining olive oil over the peppers, replace the top stem pieces, and bake, covered, until the peppers are tender, 35 minutes. Remove cover and bake another 15 minutes, or until lightly browned. Serve warm or at room temperature.

Peach Crumble

SERVES 4

8 ripe peaches, pitted and sliced
   Juice of 1 lemon
   Large pinch of ground cinnamon
   Large pinch of freshly grated nutmeg
½ cup all-purpose flour
½ cup tightly packed dark brown sugar
½ cup (1 stick) unsalted butter, chilled
   and cut into thin pieces
¼ cup quick-cooking oats
   Heavy cream (optional)

1. Preheat the oven to 375° F.

2. Arrange the peach slices in a shallow baking dish. Sprinkle with the lemon juice, cinnamon, and nutmeg.

3. In a small bowl, combine the flour and brown sugar. With your fingers, crumble the butter into the flour-sugar mixture. Stir in the oats and sprinkle the mixture on top of the sliced peaches. Bake until peaches are soft and topping is brown, about 25 minutes.

4. Serve warm with fresh or whipped cream, if desired.

I used a glass pie plate for the peach crumble; I prefer baking this type of dessert in a shallow dish so that each serving includes lots of the crumbly topping.

Skewered Shrimp and Scallops

I chose pale green Depression glass plates to serve the shrimp and scallops. The salad plate is a very rare, square Depression amethyst dessert plate, and the tall tumbler is also amethyst. The white filet tablecloth was crocheted by one of my great-aunts.

Once upon a time, I was a devoted fan of sour-lemon ice cream sodas. When I could no longer find lemon ice cream anywhere, I developed a penchant for vanilla ice cream sodas. Then, on a consultation for a wedding, I discovered fresh peach ice cream sodas. The parents of the bride-to-be served them in the garden; my client used the ripest yellow freestone peaches picked off the trees right in her orchard. I was hooked. I rushed home and immediately made sodas for Andy and me using the white Georgia Belle peaches I grow, and I continue to make them as often as possible, whenever peaches are in season.

The cool sodas are the perfect end to this slightly spicy menu. The marinated shrimps and scallops are skewered and lightly grilled or broiled. The tian of potatoes and peppers—a Provençal dish of baked, thinly sliced vegetables—can be livened up if you add one or two hot peppers in with the sweet. The tropical salsa is a wonderful combination of mangoes, papayas, avocados, and cilantro that can be made at any time of the year if your greengrocer has a good supply of imported fruits.

M E N U

SKEWERED SHRIMP AND SCALLOPS
TROPICAL SALSA
PEPPER AND POTATO TIAN
ESCAROLE SALAD WITH LIGHT CUMIN DRESSING
PEACH ICE CREAM SODAS

Skewered Shrimp and Scallops

SERVES 4

1 pound large shrimp, peeled and
   deveined, with tails left on
   Juice of 1 grapefruit
¼ cup safflower oil
1 tablespoon chopped fresh coriander
   (cilantro)
1 pound sea scallops
   Juice of 1 orange
1 tablespoon chopped fresh mint
   Salt and freshly ground black pepper

1. Place the shrimp in a glass or stainless steel bowl and add the grapefruit
juice, 2 tablespoons oil, and coriander.
Stir to mix and cover the bowl with
plastic wrap. Refrigerate for 30 minutes.

2. Place the scallops in another glass or
steel bowl and add the orange juice, remaining 2 tablespoons oil, and mint.
Stir to mix and cover the bowl with
plastic wrap. Refrigerate for 30 minutes.

3. Preheat the broiler.

4. Alternate the shrimp and scallops on
long metal skewers. Place the full skewers under the broiler for 2 minutes;
brush with a bit of the combined mari-
nades and return to the broiler. Broil
until the shrimp are slightly browned
and the scallops are done, 3 to 4 minutes longer. Season to taste and serve
immediately.

Tropical Salsa

MAKES APPROXIMATELY 1½ CUPS

½ ripe avocado, peeled
½ ripe papaya, peeled
1 ripe tomato, seeded
¼ fresh pineapple, peeled and cored
1 fresh jalapeño pepper, seeded and
   finely minced
2 scallions, trimmed and finely sliced
   Juice of ½ lemon
¼ cup olive oil
   Honey to taste (optional)

1. Finely chop the avocado, papaya, tomato, and pineapple into pieces of approximately the same size. Combine in
a medium bowl.

2. Add the remaining ingredients to the
bowl and stir well. Refrigerate until
ready to serve with the skewered
shrimp.

Pepper and Potato Tian

SERVES 4

16 green cherry peppers (1 to 1½ inches
   in diameter), seeded and sliced
   crosswise (see Note)
8 waxy potatoes, peeled and very
   thinly sliced
2 tablespoons olive oil
8 fresh marjoram leaves, torn into
   small pieces
   Salt and freshly ground black pepper

1. Preheat oven to 450°F. Butter a shallow baking dish.

2. Arrange the sliced vegetables con-
centrically in the prepared dish, alternating the slices of potato and cherry
pepper. Drizzle with the olive oil and
sprinkle the marjoram leaves on top.

3. Bake the tian for 15 to 20 minutes,
then reduce the heat to 400° F. Continue baking until the vegetables are
tender and nicely browned, approximately 15 minutes longer. Season to
taste and serve immediately.

NOTE: Use the cherry peppers if you
want a hot taste; otherwise, use 2 milder
small green bell peppers.

Escarole Salad with Light Cumin Dressing

SERVES 4

1 small head escarole, leaves torn into bite-size pieces
½ red onion, peeled and thinly sliced

Cumin Dressing
MAKES APPROXIMATELY 1 CUP
2 tablespoons safflower oil
Juice of 1 orange
Juice of ½ lime
⅛ teaspoon ground cumin
Salt and freshly ground black pepper

Zest of ½ orange
Zest of 1 lime

Place the escarole and onion in a serving bowl. Whisk the dressing ingredients together and toss with salad. Garnish with the zests right before serving.

Peach Ice Cream Sodas

SERVES 4

6 very ripe, fragrant peaches
½ cup peach or apricot nectar
4 large scoops vanilla or peach ice cream, preferably homemade
Club soda or plain seltzer
1 cup heavy cream whipped with 2 tablespoons sugar and 1 teaspoon vanilla extract

1. Peel and pit the peaches, cut into eighths. Distribute the slices evenly among 4 tall 12-ounce glasses. Add 2 tablespoons nectar to each glass and mash peaches lightly with a fork.

2. Add 1 scoop of ice cream to each glass, add the soda water or seltzer, and stir lightly to mix. Top with a dollop of flavored whipped cream and serve.

I have quite a collection of tall ice cream soda glasses in various shades of purple and green, all in the traditional Coca-Cola shape. Crocheted dresser doilies make great placemats for dessert.

Grilled Italian Sausages

I grew up in Nutley, New Jersey, on Elm Place, a street lined with maple trees and with an eclectic mix of families. Many of our neighbors were first- or second-generation immigrants, and though their backgrounds were diverse, almost all were on friendly terms. I managed to eat my way up and down the entire street, sampling Irish, English, German, French, and even Chinese cuisine.

Next-door was Mrs. Allegri, a Lithuanian woman who had become expert at her husband's Southern Italian cuisine. For Sunday dinner there was nowhere I would rather be than at their crowded table, and this menu reminds me of those days. I love to grill Italian sausages and serve them with crusty bread and sautéed vegetables. Sliced eggplant, onions, and Italian peppers are sautéed until soft in green olive oil; one could add tomatoes, zucchini, or red peppers to the mélange.

The simple salad is composed of white chicory and red leaf lettuce tossed with olive oil and a little balsamic vinegar (red wine vinegar that has been aged in oak casks—the older the better, richer, and more flavorful).

Dessert is pecan tartlets, a very American end to this immigrants' meal and, if made with frozen, uncooked individual tartlet shells, a wonderful Quick Cook cheat.

M E N U
GRILLED ITALIAN SAUSAGES
SAUTÉED EGGPLANT, ONIONS, AND PEPPERS
CHICORY AND RED LEAF SALAD
PECAN TARTLETS

Grilled Italian Sausages

SERVES 4

3 pounds hot and/or sweet Italian sausage links
6 to 8 rounds fresh sourdough bread (see Note)
   Olive oil

1. Grill the sausages over hot coals, turning frequently, until thoroughly cooked and nicely browned all over, about 10 minutes.

2. Brush both sides of the bread rounds with a bit of olive oil and place on the grill just long enough to warm the bread and make black grill lines. Serve with the hot sausages.

NOTE: I prefer small, flat individual sourdough breads for this recipe, but thick slices of sourdough loaf could be used.

Sautéed Eggplant, Onions, and Peppers

SERVES 4

8 to 12 tablespoons olive oil
2 large white onions, peeled and coarsely chopped
2 cloves garlic, peeled and minced
4 long, green Italian frying peppers, seeded and julienned
2 Japanese eggplants, cut lengthwise into ¼-inch slices
   Salt and freshly ground black pepper

1. In a large skillet, heat 4 tablespoons oil and sauté the onions and garlic until tender, 4 to 5 minutes. Add the peppers and continue to cook until they have softened, 5 minutes longer. Remove the mixture to a bowl.

2. In the same skillet, heat the remaining 4 tablespoons oil; sauté eggplant slices a few at a time just until softened, 3 to 5 minutes, adding oil as needed.

3. When all the eggplant has been sautéed, combine the vegetables, season to taste, and serve hot.

Chicory and Red Leaf Salad

SERVES 4

1 handful of a combination of white curly chicory and red leaf lettuce per person

Dressing
MAKES ¼ CUP
2 tablespoons balsamic vinegar
¼ cup olive oil
   Salt and freshly ground black pepper

Tear the greens into large pieces and arrange them on individual salad plates. Whisk together the dressing ingredients until well blended. Toss with the greens right before serving.

Pecan Tartlets

SERVES 4

4 eggs
1 cup dark brown sugar, tightly packed
¼ teaspoon salt
¼ cup molasses
¼ cup light corn syrup
3 tablespoons unsalted butter
   Grated rind of ½ lemon
   Grated rind of ½ orange
1½ cups chopped pecans
4 uncooked 4½-inch Tart Shells (page 11)
1 cup perfect pecan halves

Frozen tartlet shells, 4½ inches in diameter, make it quite possible to serve fresh pecan pies for dessert; the crème fraîche flavored with lemon and orange zests complements the sweetness of the pecan filling.

Lemon-Orange Crème Fraîche
  ¾ cup Crème Fraîche (page 11)
  ½ tablespoon lemon zest
  ½ tablespoon orange zest

1. Preheat the oven to 325° F.

2. Place the eggs in a mixing bowl and beat with a fork. Blend in the brown sugar, salt, molasses, and corn syrup. Heat the butter until just melted; stir into sugar mixture with citrus rinds, mixing until thoroughly blended. Add the chopped pecans.

3. Pour the filling mixture into the pastry shells and neatly arrange the pecan halves on top. Bake until the pastry is lightly browned and the filling set, approximately 30 minutes. Remove from the oven and let cool.

4. While the tartlets are baking, beat the crème fraîche with a mixer at high speed until thick and fluffy. Quickly blend in the zests and chill until ready to serve with the tartlets.

Pasta with Swiss Chard, Eggplant, and Mushrooms

My Nashville friend Salli La Grone introduced me to myriad uses for the Jerusalem artichoke. It makes a very fine relish, is delicious pureed, sautéed, and even raw—if thinly sliced—and is especially wonderful in soup. This recipe was one of Salli's favorites, and it has become one of mine. The Jerusalem artichoke, by the way, is a very close relative of the sunflower, but it is cultivated only for its potatolike tuber. It is easy to grow—I planted a few one spring and the following October had an immense underground crop. The next year the harvest was three times the size of the first, and as the roots spread like wildfire, my artichoke patch soon threatened to overcome the garden.

While I make my artichoke-patrol trips around the garden, I like to gather a basketful of vegetables with which to concoct a pasta sauce. This combination was a result of one such walk: I found Swiss chard and eggplants, then added mushrooms. One could also use spinach or arugula, peppers, fennel, celery root, squashes, and beans. I generally cook each of the vegetables separately and then combine them for last-minute sautéeing with herbs and spices.

Clafouti is a French dessert—a batter baked over a base of fruit, usually cherries, plums, or peaches. Made with cranberries, in individual baking cups, this clafouti is sweet-sour and a wonderful end to this country meal.

My daughter, Alexis, inherited my maternal grandmother's collection of Fiestaware; we have filled the gaps with dinner and salad plates and some other unusual pieces so that now we can serve dinner for twenty. This meal begins with Jerusalem artichoke soup, which looks best in a bright orange Fiesta bowl set atop a bright yellow plate. A small juice glass is used for wine.

MENU

JERUSALEM ARTICHOKE SOUP
PASTA WITH SWISS CHARD, EGGPLANT, AND MUSHROOMS
CRANBERRY CLAFOUTI CUPS

Jerusalem Artichoke Soup

SERVES 6 TO 8

3 pounds Jerusalem artichokes, peeled
   and sliced
¾ cup (1½ sticks) unsalted butter
4 medium onions, peeled and sliced
2 ripe pears, peeled, cored, and cut
   into chunks
4 cups water
4 cups milk
   Salt and freshly ground black pepper
   Pinch of sugar
   Julienned strips of tomato

1. In a large, heavy saucepan, sauté the Jerusalem artichokes in butter until soft, approximately 7 minutes. Add the onions and cook until soft, approximately 5 minutes longer.

2. Add the pears and water to the saucepan. Bring to a boil, reduce heat, and simmer 30 minutes.

3. In a food processor, puree the soup in 2-cup batches until smooth. Return the pureed mixture to the saucepan.

4. Add the milk; season to taste with salt, pepper, and sugar. Heat gently (do not boil) and serve garnished with julienned strips of tomato and a sprinkling of pepper.

This vegetarian menu was designed especially for Alexis: the main course is a pasta with Swiss chard, eggplant, and mushrooms, served on a rare oversized Fiesta charger.

Pasta with Swiss Chard, Eggplant, and Mushrooms

SERVES 6

½ cup olive oil
1 pound fresh Swiss chard, trimmed,
   washed, and cut into 1-inch crosswise
   pieces
6 tiny (2-to 3-inch) eggplants, trimmed
   and cut diagonally into ½-inch slices
2 cloves garlic, peeled and sliced
   lengthwise

2 large fresh wild mushrooms (we used
   shiitake), trimmed and sliced
1 pound small, ear-shape pasta (we
   used orecchiette basesi)
¼ to ½ cup extra-virgin (green)
   olive oil
½ cup diced fresh mozzarella cheese
½ cup crumbled Gorgonzola cheese
   Salt and freshly ground black pepper
   Freshly grated Parmesan cheese

1. In a large skillet, heat 2 tablespoons olive oil and sauté the Swiss chard for 2 minutes. Remove from the skillet and set aside.

2. Add 2 tablespoons olive oil to the skillet, heat, and sauté the eggplants and garlic for 2 to 3 minutes. Add the mushrooms and sauté until well browned, 7 to 9 minutes. Add the sautéed Swiss chard and cook for 1 more minute.

3. While the vegetables are being sautéed, cook the pasta in a large pot of boiling water until done, 8 to 10 minutes. Drain well and toss with a bit of

the extra-virgin olive oil to prevent the pasta from sticking together.

4. Toss the hot pasta immediately with the mozzarella and Gorgonzola and a bit more extra-virgin olive oil. Toss in the sautéed vegetables, season to taste, top with grated cheese, and drizzle with additional olive oil, as desired. Serve immediately.

Cranberry Clafouti Cups

SERVES 6

3 cups fresh cranberries
1½ cups cranberry juice cocktail or water
6 eggs
1 cup plus 2 tablespoons sugar
6 tablespoons all-purpose flour
1 cup plus 2 tablespoons milk
¾ cup heavy cream
¾ teaspoon vanilla extract
Pinch of ground cinnamon

1. Preheat oven to 400° F. Butter 6 1-cup custard cups or a 9-inch oven-proof baking dish.

2. In a small saucepan, cook the cranberries and cranberry juice over low heat for 5 minutes. Drain the cranberries, reserving both berries and juice. Return the juice to the saucepan and boil down until reduced to ¼ cup.

3. Combine the eggs, sugar, flour, milk, cream, and vanilla in a blender and blend at high speed for 1 minute, scraping down the sides of the jar once. Stir in the reduced cranberry liquid.

4. Spread the cranberries in the bottom of the prepared dishes. Pour the custard mixture over the berries and sprinkle with cinnamon. Bake until custard is puffed and golden, 40 to 45 minutes. Serve hot or warm.

I baked these individual cranberry clafoutis in footed custard cups set in a bain-marie and served them atop more of Alexis's Fiestaware.

Barbecued Ribs

This is a really good menu to have outdoors on a warm fall day. We covered the picnic table with newspaper, brought out all the old white enamel bowls and pots, and served an informal lunch that was as memorable as the day itself.

The shrimps are steamed in their shells over a mixture of beer and lemon juice; sprinkle them with extra seafood seasoning and a bit of cayenne pepper if you like a spicier taste. Choose very fresh large or extra-large shrimps, and take care not to overcook them. In our house, the rule when cooking shrimps or soft-boiled eggs is to use a very loud timer and let nothing distract one. Too many shrimps have been cooked to ruin, too many eggs hard-boiled or exploded because of a momentary distraction.

I'm very fond of barbecued ribs, and I hate to see them blackened and dried up by too much time on the grill. I've found that an initial poaching cuts the grilling time by half and keeps the ribs juicy and succulent, while at the same time remove much of the fattiness.

The wild blueberry ice is a lovely, fresh-tasting—and very easy—end to a satisfying meal.

M E N U

SHRIMP STEAMED WITH BEER AND SPICES
BARBECUED RIBS
CORN SOUFFLÉ
DANDELION GREENS SALAD
WILD BLUEBERRY ICE

Preceding page:
*This messy meal of
steamed shrimp and
barbecued ribs was
served outdoors, on
a newsprint-covered
table (brown paper
would do just as
well). The dishes
are white enamel-
ware, the flatware
is plastic-handled,
and the relishes
are served right out
of their old blue-
glass canning jars.*

Shrimp Steamed with Beer and Spices

SERVES 2

1 (12-ounce) can of beer
Approximately 1 tablespoon seafood
  seasoning, preferably Old Bay
Juice of 1 lemon
1 pound large shrimp, unpeeled

1. In a large saucepan, combine the beer, seafood seasoning to taste, and lemon juice. Bring to a boil.

2. Place the shrimp in a steamer basket, place basket in saucepan, cover, and steam shrimp over the liquid just until they are pink and done, 3 to 5 minutes. (The shrimp can also be boiled right in the liquid.)

3. Remove the shrimp from the pan and serve hot, warm, or cold.

Barbecued Ribs

SERVES 2

Barbecue Sauce
MAKES APPROXIMATELY 1½ CUPS
  2 tablespoons olive oil
  1 onion, peeled and chopped
  1 large clove garlic, peeled and minced
  1 rib celery, chopped
  1 cup ketchup
  ¼ cup red wine vinegar
  ¼ cup dark brown sugar, tightly packed
  1 tablespoon Dijon mustard
  2 tablespoons Worcestershire sauce

1½ pounds baby back ribs

1. To make the sauce, heat the olive oil in a heavy saucepan and sauté the onion, garlic, and celery until tender but not browned, about 5 minutes. Add the remaining ingredients and cook

over low heat for at least 10 minutes. Puree the mixture in a food processor until smooth. Let cool slightly.

2. Poach the ribs in a large pot of simmering water for 5 minutes. Drain and baste both sides generously with the barbecue sauce.

3. Grill the ribs over hot coals for 5 to 7 minutes; turn them over, baste, and grill until done but still juicy, 7 to 10 minutes longer. Serve hot, warm, or cold with additional barbecue sauce.

Corn Soufflé

SERVES 2

3 to 4 ears of corn, husked
3 tablespoons unsalted butter
2 scallions, finely minced
⅓ cup all-purpose flour
¾ cup milk
3 eggs, yolks lightly beaten and whites
  beaten until dry
  Salt and freshly ground black pepper

1. Preheat the oven to 350° F. Butter a 5- or 6-cup charlotte mold or soufflé dish and set aside.

2. Cut the kernels from the ears of corn with a sharp knife. (You should do this over a bowl to catch any of the starchy white milk from the corn.) Go back over the cobs and scrape out as much milk as possible; you should have 2 cups of kernels and liquid.

3. In a large skillet, melt the butter and sauté the kernels, their liquid, and the scallions for 3 minutes. Add the flour and blend thoroughly. Stir in the milk, whisking to break up any lumps of flour. Season to taste and cook for 2 to 3 minutes.

4. Remove the mixture from the heat and let cool 10 minutes. Beat in the egg yolks, then gently but thoroughly fold in the beaten egg whites.

5. Pour the batter into the prepared dish and bake until puffed and golden, 20 to 25 minutes. Serve immediately.

Dandelion Greens Salad

SERVES 2

1 handful of torn dandelion greens per person

Dressing
MAKES ¼ CUP
  1 tablespoon fresh lemon juice
  1 tablespoon white wine vinegar
  ⅛ teaspoon grated lemon rind
  1 shallot, peeled and finely chopped
  1 teaspoon coarse-grain mustard
     Salt and freshly ground black pepper

Place the greens in a serving bowl. Whisk together all ingredients for the dressing. Toss the dandelion greens with the dressing right before serving.

Wild Blueberry Ice

MAKES 1 PINT

  1 (15-ounce) can wild blueberries in heavy syrup
  ½ cup water
  ¼ cup sugar

1. Drain the syrup from the blueberries and reserve in a bowl. In a small saucepan, combine the water and sugar; cook over low heat until the sugar dissolves. Add the sugar syrup and one-third of the blueberries to the blueberry syrup. Chill thoroughly.

2. Freeze the mixture in an ice-cream maker according to the manufacturer's directions.

3. Serve a scoop of blueberry ice with the reserved blueberries.

The wild blueberry ice, made from those tiny, flavorful wild Maine blueberries, looks unbelievably colorful on a white enamel plate with a few loose berries as a simple garnish.

Black Bass with Balsamic Vinegar

David Bouley, the chef-cum-owner of New York's chic restaurant Bouley, was one of the first to popularize the use of black bass fillets as a dinner entrée. The Chinese have served black bass fried and sweet and sour for a long time, but the fish was always considered too bony to fillet and too common to glorify. Black bass, however, happens to be a succulent and delicious fish, and prepared as in this menu, it proves a fine addition to any cook's repertoire.

I have chosen to serve the bass with warm soba noodles garnished with a julienne of cucumbers and with long Chinese string beans. The radicchio salad is very colorful, and the orange-flavored dressing goes well with the fish.

I love mango and try to eat one every day when they are in season. They remind me of a trip we took to Haiti, where the trees along the roadsides are laden for months of the year with thousands of sweet, green, orange-fleshed fruit. In the dessert for this dinner, the flesh of the mango is peeled and cut off the pit in chunks, then served with fresh raspberries and sprigs of fresh mint. A good, ripe mango is juicy enough to serve with nothing but this simple garnish.

About five years ago, I found a beautiful copper luster dinner service at a tag sale; though they are probably American, they have a rather Oriental appearance and make an apt setting for this dish of black bass with soba noodles. Imari teacups, blue and white fabrics, and a feather fan complete the exotic setting.

MENU

BLACK BASS WITH BALSAMIC VINEGAR
SOBA NOODLES WITH CUCUMBERS
BLANCHED CHINESE LONG BEANS
RED AND ORANGE SALAD
MANGO WITH RASPBERRIES AND MINT

Black Bass with Balsamic Vinegar

SERVES 2

¼ cup balsamic vinegar
2 tablespoons (¼ stick) unsalted butter
2 (⅓–½ pound) black bass fillets

1. In a skillet large enough to hold the fillets, combine the vinegar and butter and reduce the mixture by one-half over medium-low heat.

2. Add the black bass fillets and sauté for 5 minutes, turning once while cooking. Serve immediately with the vinegar sauce in pan.

Soba Noodles with Cucumbers

SERVES 2

8 ounces Japanese soba (buckwheat) noodles
½ small Kirby cucumber
¼ cup soy sauce
8 drops hot pepper oil
1 tablespoon white vinegar
½ teaspoon finely minced fresh ginger
¼ cup oriental sesame oil
Black sesame seeds

1. Cook the noodles in a large pot of boiling water until tender, approximately 5 minutes. Drain well.

2. Peel the cucumber and remove the seeds with a sharp spoon or a melon-ball scoop. Julienne the flesh into long, thin pieces, and set aside.

3. Whisk together the soy sauce, pepper oil, vinegar, ginger, and sesame oil; toss with the warm noodles. Gently mix in the julienned cucumber and top with the sesame seeds. Serve at room temperature or slightly chilled.

Blanched Chinese Long Beans

SERVES 2

¾ pound fresh Chinese long green beans
Salt and freshly ground black pepper

1. Blanch the beans in a large pot of boiling water until tender, 4 to 5 minutes. Drain well.

2. While still hot, divide the beans into 2 bunches and coil loosely on side plates or shallow bowls. Season to taste and serve immediately.

Red and Orange Salad

SERVES 2

½ head radicchio, leaves halved
½ head Treviso radicchio
½ cup red seedless grapes, approximately

Dressing
MAKES APPROXIMATELY ¼ CUP
1 tablespoon safflower oil
1 teaspoon soy sauce
Juice of ½ orange
Zest of ½ orange

Combine both types of radicchio in a serving bowl with the grapes. Whisk together all the ingredients for the dressing and toss with the radicchio and grapes right before serving.

Mango with Raspberries and Mint

SERVES 2

1 ripe, firm mango, carefully peeled
½ cup fresh whole red raspberries
Sprigs of fresh mint

1. With a sharp knife, carefully slice 6 to 8 wedges of mango, keeping the pieces as uniform in size as possible and avoiding the large elongated pit in the center.

2. Place 3 or 4 mango wedges on each dessert plate. Spoon the raspberries around the mango and garnish with a sprig of fresh mint.

Chicken Cacciatore

The standard recipe for chicken cacciatore requires stewing the chicken for a rather long time in a rich, spicy red sauce, then serving it with broad egg noodles or fettuccine. In my recipe, the cut-up chicken marinates a while (overnight is best, but 30 minutes will do in a pinch) and is grilled over coals right before serving. I have tried broiling the chicken and grilling on a gas grill, but I prefer outdoor grilling over hickory or mesquite. Be very careful not to blacken the chicken—it is better to cook it slowly than to burn it to a crisp.

Angel-hair pasta is so called because it is the finest, thinnest pasta. It cooks very quickly and must not be overcooked or it will become a sticky, tangled mass. I cook it right before serving and try to toss it immediately with whatever light sauce or flavoring I have prepared.

This salad is a variation of one I ate at Il Cantinori, a New York restaurant. Fresh celery, onions, and ripe plum tomatoes are a very good combination—in fact, celery is underused as a salad ingredient. The dressing is a tangy mixture of oil, balsamic vinegar, and heavy cream, flavored with chopped or shredded fresh basil.

Early fall is the time for the very finest fresh, ripe peaches, and I try to take full advantage of their availability. I make peach preserves, peach chutneys, whole spiced peaches, lots of peach pies and tarts, and poached or baked peaches. Perhaps my favorite is this recipe for champagne-poached peaches; it is very easy, and the result—if you use good peaches—is extraordinary.

To serve this simple chicken cacciatore, I borrowed some English china from Amanda, my assistant. The pressed glass candlesticks and machine-woven lace napkins are my own; the tablecloth is one of the nicest in my collection— hand-loomed flax in its original condition, never laundered, the fringed edges are still shiny and untangled.

M E N U

ANGEL-HAIR PASTA WITH PARMESAN
CHICKEN CACCIATORE
TOMATO, SWEET ONION, AND CELERY SALAD
CHAMPAGNE-POACHED PEACHES

Angel-Hair Pasta with Parmesan

SERVES 3 TO 4

8 ounces angel-hair pasta
4 tablespoons (½ stick) unsalted butter
2 cloves garlic, peeled and thinly sliced
3 tablespoons flat Italian parsley leaves
  Salt and freshly ground black pepper
⅓ cup very thin Parmesan cheese slices

1. Cook the pasta according to package directions. Drain well and set aside in a warm place.

2. In a medium skillet, melt the butter and sauté the garlic over very low heat for 5 minutes. Add the parsley and cook for 1 to 2 minutes. Toss immediately with the pasta and season with salt and pepper. Top with thin slivers of Parmesan cheese (cut with a very sharp cheese knife) and serve.

Opposite: *I
poached these
peaches in a tin-
lined copper
pot, one from
my lifelong
accumulation of
cookware from
visits to Europe.*

Chicken Cacciatore

SERVES 3 TO 4

Marinade

    1 (6-ounce) can tomato paste
    ½ cup olive oil
    ¼ cup red wine vinegar
    ⅓ cup red wine
    ½ teaspoon cayenne pepper
    ¼ teaspoon red pepper flakes
    ½ teaspoon salt
    ½ teaspoon freshly ground black pepper
    1 teaspoon Cajun spice for chicken
      (optional)

    1 (3-pound) chicken, cut into 8 pieces
      Salt and freshly ground black pepper

1. The day before, combine marinade ingredients, mixing well. Place the chicken pieces in a large, shallow baking dish. Pour the marinade over the chicken and let sit overnight in the refrigerator.

2. The next day, preheat the broiler or prepare a hot grill with coals and a fragrant wood. (Hickory or mesquite is wonderful with the chicken.)

3. Broil (or grill) the chicken pieces for 8 to 10 minutes, turn over, and baste with the marinade. Cook 8 to 10 minutes longer or until done. Season to taste and serve hot.

Tomato, Sweet Onion, and Celery Salad

SERVES 3 TO 4

    2 ripe red plum tomatoes, cut into
      ¼-inch slices
    1 sweet onion (preferably Vidalia),
      peeled and cut into ⅛-inch slices
    3 ribs celery, cut crosswise into thin
      pieces, leaves left whole

Dressing
MAKES ¾ CUP
    ¼ cup olive oil
    3 tablespoons balsamic vinegar
    2 tablespoons finely chopped fresh basil
    2 tablespoons heavy cream
      Salt and freshly ground black pepper

Arrange the vegetables on individual salad plates and set aside. Whisk olive oil with the vinegar. Add basil and heavy cream. Season to taste and pour over the vegetables. Serve immediately.

Champagne-poached Peaches

SERVES 3 TO 4

    2 cups Champagne (either flat or
      bubbly) or good dry white wine
    2 tablespoons framboise (raspberry
      liqueur)
    ⅔ cup sugar
    1 vanilla bean, split lengthwise
    6 small, ripe (but firm) peaches
    ½ cup Crème Fraîche
      (page 11) or heavy cream
    1 teaspoon sugar
    ½ teaspoon vanilla extract

1. Combine Champagne, framboise, sugar, and vanilla bean in a large, deep kettle and bring to a boil.

2. Reduce heat to a simmer, add peaches, and poach until tender but not soft, 5 to 10 minutes. Remove from heat and let the peaches cool a bit in the liquid. Drain.

3. Whip the crème fraîche with sugar and vanilla until it forms soft peaks. Spoon over the peaches (chilled or room temperature) and serve.

NOTE: Plums and apricots are also excellent cooked this way.

Baked Scallops with Orange Sections

I like to be in Martha's Vineyard in the fall during the scallop harvest—it is wonderful to get the shellfish freshly shucked, sometimes with the bright coral roe still attached. Sea scallops are approximately 1½ inches in diameter, should be very sweet smelling, and are white or shell-pink in color. Bay scallops are about half an inch in diameter, are usually bluish white, and should also smell sweet.

The lemon-chive pasta was invented by my assistant Amanda O'Brien. We have found that almost all of the flavored pastas are more tender and delicate in texture if made by hand rather than in the food processor. It does take a bit longer this way, but the result is generally worth the time.

The pasta and scallops need just a few vegetables and a small, flavorful salad. I like watercress with toasted hazelnuts. Using an oil that picks up the flavor of the nuts in a recipe is a good idea, but be sure that the nut oil is impeccably fresh and don't use too much of it—all nut oils will overpower a salad if used heavily.

The tropical fruit plate can combine any number of the exotic varieties that are available at this time of year. I used a West Indian papaya, carambolas, and some bright Mineolas—extra-sweet, seedless oranges.

American Hobnail was a sturdy, popular pattern of Depression glass; I particularly like it in this very pale blue. With the pale blue damask cloth and the pearl-handled flatware, it makes a lovely setting for these baked scallops.

M E N U

BAKED SCALLOPS WITH ORANGE SECTIONS
LEMON-CHIVE PASTA
BABY GREEN AND YELLOW SQUASH
WATERCRESS SALAD WITH HAZELNUT DRESSING
TROPICAL FRUIT

Baked Scallops with Orange Sections

SERVES 3

¾ *pound large sea scallops*
2 *teaspoons olive oil, approximately*
2 *navel oranges, carefully peeled*
¾ *pound small bay scallops*
1 *tablespoon chopped fresh dill*

1. Preheat the oven to 450° F.

2. Put the sea scallops in a 9-inch baking dish and drizzle with olive oil.

3. Using a small, sharp knife, carefully cut the orange sections from the white membrane over the baking dish so that juice is saved; using your hands, squeeze out all remaining juice from the membranes over the dish. Arrange the orange sections among the scallops and bake for 8 minutes.

4. Remove the baking dish from the oven and turn the heat to broil.

5. Add the remaining bay scallops to the dish and sprinkle with dill. Broil just until all scallops are cooked, 3 to 4 minutes. Serve immediately.

Lemon-Chive Pasta

SERVES 3

Pasta
3½ cups all-purpose flour
1 teaspoon salt
5 eggs
1 tablespoon olive oil
2 tablespoons finely chopped fresh chives
Grated zest of 1 lemon

Sauce
2 tablespoons (¼ stick) unsalted butter
1 tablespoon chopped fresh chives
2 tablespoons olive oil
Zest of ½ lemon
Salt and freshly ground white pepper

1. To make the pasta, combine the flour and salt on a large, flat board. Make a well in the center and break the eggs into it; add the olive oil, chives, and lemon zest. Gently incorporate all ingredients with a fork, then knead the dough with the heels of your hands until smooth, approximately 5 minutes. (If the dough seems a little sticky, add a bit more flour.)

2. Using a pasta machine, roll out the dough to the desired thickness. Set the machine to fettuccine width and pass the noodles through it. Store well wrapped in freezer until ready to use.

3. In a small skillet, heat the butter and sauté the chives lightly for a minute or two. Add 1 tablespoon olive oil and the lemon zest, and sauté quickly for 1 minute. Do not let the mixture brown.

4. Cook the pasta in large pot of boiling water just until tender, 3 to 5 minutes. Drain well and toss immediately with the remaining 1 tablespoon olive oil.

5. Toss the pasta with the butter and chive mixture and season to taste. Serve immediately.

NOTE: You may find this yields more pasta than you need. The excess pasta can be frozen successfully in an airtight container or plastic bag. It will need to be cooked a bit longer, 4 to 6 minutes.

Baby Green and Yellow Squash

SERVES 3

½ pound miniature pattypan squash
1 tablespoon unsalted butter, melted
Salt and freshly ground black pepper

Wash and halve the squash and blanch them until tender in a large pot of boiling water, 3 to 5 minutes. Drain. Toss the squash with butter and season to taste. Serve immediately.

Watercress Salad with Hazelnut Dressing

SERVES 3

1 bunch fresh watercress, washed and dried with tough stems removed
2 tablespoons hazelnut oil
1 tablespoon Champagne vinegar
Salt and freshly ground black pepper
¼ cup toasted and skinned hazelnuts (see Note, page 65)

Place the watercress in a serving bowl. Whisk together the oil and vinegar until well blended. Season to taste. Drizzle the oil and vinegar mixture over the watercress and toss lightly. Top with the whole hazelnuts and serve immediately.

Tropical Fruit

SERVES 3

2 sweet, seedless oranges, preferably Mineolas, peeled and cut crosswise into ¼-inch slices

1 ripe papaya, peeled and cut crosswise into ¼-inch slices

2 star fruits (carambola), cut crosswise into ¼-inch slices

Arrange the sliced fruit on individual dessert plates and serve immediately.

A simple fruit salad can be a startlingly beautiful—and delicious—dessert, especially when served on well-chosen china, like this pale blue opaline plate. The carambolas are an unexpected touch: people are always surprised at their perfect star shape and their lemon-lime flavor. (When serving papaya, do not discard the seeds; they are edible, and delicious.)

Lobster with Champagne Dipping Sauce

This is a wonderful menu that combines several of my favorite foods: lobster, gnocchi, asparagus, and crêpes. The lobsters are first poached, cooled slightly, split lengthwise, and then broiled or grilled over fragrant coals. The combination of poaching and broiling ensures that the meat is fully cooked yet succulent and flavorful; do be careful with the last stage, though, since lobster can easily overcook and become dry. The champagne dipping sauce is like a beurre blanc, but heavy cream is used in place of butter. It is very easy to prepare and maintains its texture beautifully.

The herb gnocchi are made from a base of *pâte à choux* to which is added mashed potatoes, cheese, and herbs. Small, round logs are poached, then baked with more cheese and butter.

Crêpes are a very good Quick Cook dessert. They can be made in advance and frozen in stacks, and I have found that the microwave does an excellent job of thawing and warming them. When they are served with fresh lemon and lime juice and a sprinkling of sugar and garnished with glacéed cape gooseberries, they make a most elegant dessert.

For this lobster menu, I chose sea-green Depression glass plates, which contrast beautifully with the shell-pink linens. The flatware, an unusual and little-known pattern made by Herbert Robinson and C. B. Barrie, was a lovely surprise: I found it while clearing out an old house I had bought here in Westport.

M E N U

LOBSTER WITH CHAMPAGNE DIPPING SAUCE
HERB GNOCCHI
PENCIL ASPARAGUS WITH LEMON
LEMON-LIME CRÊPES WITH GLACÉED GOOSEBERRIES

Lobster with Champagne Dipping Sauce

SERVES 4

Champagne Dipping Sauce
MAKES 1¼ TO 1½ CUPS
  1 bouquet garni (see Note)
  ¾ cup Champagne
  4 shallots, peeled and finely minced
     Salt and freshly ground white pepper
  1 cup heavy cream

  2 (1½-pound) live lobsters
  5 tablespoons olive oil
  1 tablespoon Champagne vinegar
  1 small head limestone lettuce, leaves
     separated, washed, and dried
  1 small head red leaf lettuce, leaves
     separated, washed, and dried

1. To make dipping sauce, combine the bouquet garni, Champagne, and shallots in a large saucepan. Bring to a boil, reduce the heat, and let simmer for 5 minutes. Strain the mixture into a clean skillet, stir in the cream, and reduce by one-half over medium-low heat. Season to taste.

2. Preheat the broiler.

3. In a large pot of boiling water, poach the lobsters for 5 minutes. Remove and let cool slightly.

4. With a very sharp knife, halve the poached lobsters lengthwise. Place each half, cut side up, in a shallow baking dish and brush with ½ tablespoon olive oil. Broil until cooked through, approximately 5 minutes.

5. Whisk together 3 tablespoons oil with the vinegar and toss with the lettuce leaves. Divide the lettuce among the dinner plates and place a lobster half on top of each. Serve with the Champagne Dipping Sauce.

NOTE: A bouquet garni (a small cheesecloth bag filled with herbs and spices) can be made of almost any combination, but for this I recommend 4 sprigs of fresh parsley, 1 fresh bay leaf, and ½ teaspoon fresh thyme leaves.

Herb Gnocchi

SERVES 4

Pâte à choux
  ½ cup water
  3 tablespoons unsalted butter, cut into
     small pieces
  ½ teaspoon salt
     Pinch of freshly ground black pepper
     Small pinch of freshly grated nutmeg
  6 tablespoons all-purpose flour
  2 eggs

  3 to 4 baking potatoes (1 pound),
     peeled, quartered, and boiled until
     tender
  ⅓ cup grated Swiss or Parmesan cheese
  ¾ cup finely chopped fresh chervil,
     parsley, or basil
     Salt and freshly ground black pepper
  4 tablespoons (½ stick) unsalted butter
  ½ cup freshly grated Parmesan cheese

1. To make the *pâte à choux*, combine the water, butter, salt, pepper, and nutmeg in a large saucepan and bring to a boil; cook gently until the butter has melted.

2. Remove the saucepan from the heat and add the flour, beating vigorously with a wooden spoon until blended.

3. Return the saucepan to moderately high heat, stirring continuously until the mixture leaves the sides of the pan, forming a mass and slightly coating the bottom of the pan, about 1 to 2 minutes. Remove from the heat.

4. Make a well in the center of the mixture and beat in the eggs, one at a time, until combined. Stir a minute longer to blend well. Set aside.

5. In a large bowl, mash the drained potatoes with a fork or potato masher or put them through a ricer. Stir in 1 cup *pâte à choux,* ⅓ cup cheese, and the herbs. Season to taste.

6. Roll the dough into an even log about 1 inch in diameter, then cut into 1½-inch lengths.

7. Fill a 12-inch skillet with lightly salted simmering water and add the gnocchi. Poach gently for 15 to 20 minutes. When they have almost doubled in size and turn easily in the water, they are done. Drain on paper towels.

8. About 15 minutes before serving, preheat the broiler. Lightly butter a shallow baking dish.

9. Place the gnocchi in the prepared dish, dot with the butter, and sprinkle with the Parmesan cheese. Brown slowly under a moderately hot broiler for 10 minutes and serve immediately.

Pencil Asparagus with Lemon

SERVES 4

1 pound fresh, pencil-thin green
   asparagus, trimmed to equal lengths
   Salt and freshly ground black pepper
   Fresh lemon wedges

Blanch the asparagus in a large pot of boiling water until just tender and bright green, 3 to 5 minutes. Drain well and serve immediately with salt, pepper, and lemon wedges.

Lemon-Lime Crêpes with Glacéed Gooseberries

SERVES 4

Batter
MAKES APPROXIMATELY TWELVE 6-INCH CRÊPES
1¼ cups all-purpose flour
  4 eggs
  1 cup milk
1¼ cups cold water
  3 tablespoons unsalted butter, melted
  ½ teaspoon salt

  1 pint fresh cape gooseberries
  1 cup granulated sugar
  ⅓ cup water

  ¼ cup confectioners' sugar
     Fresh lemons and limes

1. Mix batter ingredients at high speed in a blender or food processor for 30 seconds; scrape down the sides and blend 30 seconds longer. Refrigerate for at least 30 minutes.

2. Gently tear down the papery skins of the gooseberries to form petal-like leaves on each. Set aside.

3. In a heavy skillet, combine the granulated sugar and the water over medium heat. Swirl the pan until the sugar dissolves; do not stir. Let the syrup boil until it reaches hard-ball stage (300° F.).

4. Holding the gooseberries by the "petals," carefully dip them in the syrup to coat completely. Set them on a lightly oiled cookie sheet to cool and harden.

5. Pour approximately ¼ cup batter into a hot, buttered crêpe pan or onto a hot, buttered griddle. Cook over medium-high heat until the surface becomes bubbly; carefully flip the crêpe and cook until golden brown, 30 seconds longer. Remove from the pan.

6. Sprinkle each crêpe with lemon and lime juice. Fold, dust with sugar, and serve with the glacéed gooseberries.

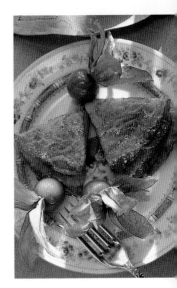

I served the dessert crêpes on plates from my sister Laura's collection of twentieth-century English floral china; the glacéed cape gooseberries look like little flyaway paper lanterns.

Pork Tenderloin

My brother Frank loves pork, and when he was visiting recently from South Carolina, our sister Kathy Evans made this menu for a get-together. The tenderloin—or boneless loin—of pork is rendered even more tender by a short, dry marinade; the onion-raisin conserve, flavored with fresh tangerine juice, is an excellent accompaniment.

Bulgur—wheat that has been cooked, dried, and coarsely ground—is a staple grain in the Middle East that is becoming more common in this country. It must be soaked (follow package directions), but you need not cook it at all: just enhance the flavor by adding vegetables, herbs, and spices and serve it hot, warm, or cold as a salad.

The sauté of cabbage, onions, and Granny Smith apples is pretty as well as tasty. Green cabbage can be substituted, but I prefer the color and taste of red for this autumnal menu. If you like, add a small glass of red wine after the cabbage has been cooking for 3 or 4 minutes.

I freeze a few small bags of pumpkin puree—about a half cup in each—every fall so I can make this dessert throughout the winter. It's basically a cup custard with pumpkin and spices added, and I like to serve it with a dark and flavorful gingerbread. The cake can be baked ahead and frozen, but it is so easy and so very good fresh out of the oven.

MENU

PORK TENDERLOIN
BULGUR WITH MUSHROOMS
RED CABBAGE WITH APPLES
PUMPKIN CUSTARD
GINGER CAKE

*Preceding page:
This pork
tenderloin with
onion-raisin
conserve is a family
favorite; I served it
on a blue and
orange antique
Spode dinner service
whose Japanese-
inspired pattern
looks very good
on a woven cloth
I found on a trip
to Japan. The wine
goblets are amber
Depression glass;
the forks are by C.
B. Barker.*

Pork Tenderloin

SERVES 4

1   (2¼-pound) pork tenderloin
½   teaspoon coarse salt
½   teaspoon freshly ground black pepper
5   bay leaves (preferably fresh)
3   sprigs fresh thyme
2   tablespoons olive oil
¼   cup fresh tangerine or orange juice

Onion-Raisin Conserve
½   cup raisins
½   cup fresh tangerine or orange juice
3   tablespoons unsalted butter
½   red onion, peeled, halved, and thinly
    sliced lengthwise
1   small bulb fennel, halved, cored, and
    thinly sliced lengthwise
1   teaspoon sugar
    Salt and freshly ground black pepper

1. Place the tenderloin in a baking dish and rub with the salt, pepper, bay leaves, and thyme. Let rest at room temperature for 30 minutes.

2. Preheat oven to 375° F.

3. Scrape the marinade off the pork; reserve. Heat the olive oil in a large skillet and add the tenderloin. Sear the meat quickly over high heat until well browned on all sides.

4. Place the seared meat in a foil-lined roasting pan. Rub the reserved marinade back onto the meat and pour tangerine juice over it. Tightly close the foil and cook for 20 minutes. Remove the tenderloin from the oven and loosen the foil to allow any steam to escape. Return to the oven for 30 to 40 minutes, or until the meat registers 160° F. on a thermometer. Let rest at least 10 minutes before slicing.

5. While the tenderloin is roasting, make the conserve. Combine the raisins and the tangerine or orange juice and let macerate 30 minutes.

6. Melt 2 tablespoons of the butter in a large skillet and sauté the onion slowly for 5 minutes. When the onion has softened, add the fennel. Cook over medium heat for 5 minutes. Add the raisins, juice, and the remaining 1 tablespoon butter. Stir in sugar and season to taste.

7. Cut the tenderloin into slices and serve with the warm conserve.

Bulgur with Mushrooms

SERVES 4

1   cup bulgur (cracked wheat)
1   cup warm Veal or Beef Stock
    (page 13)
1   tablespoon olive oil
3   tablespoons unsalted butter
6   button mushrooms, trimmed and
    sliced
1   large shallot, peeled and finely
    minced
1   tablespoon fresh thyme
    Salt and freshly ground black pepper

1. Combine the bulgur and stock in a bowl and let soak until tender, approximately 45 minutes. After soaking, place the bulgur in a sieve and let the excess stock drain off.

2. In a medium skillet, combine the olive oil and 1 tablespoon butter; sauté the mushrooms until well browned, about 10 minutes.

3. In a large skillet, melt the remaining butter and sauté the shallot until tender but not browned, about 5 minutes. Add the bulgur and thyme and heat thoroughly. Add the mushrooms and season to taste. Serve hot.

Red Cabbage with Apples

SERVES 4

½ cup (1 stick) unsalted butter
1 large onion, peeled and thinly sliced lengthwise
2 cloves garlic, peeled and finely minced
1 head red cabbage, cored and cut into 1-inch-wide strips
2 Granny Smith apples, cored and cut into wedges

1. In a large skillet, melt the butter. Add the onion and garlic and sauté until softened, about 5 minutes.

2. Add the cabbage to the skillet and cook until tender but still crisp, 4 to 5 minutes. Add the apples and cook just until soft but not mushy, 2 to 4 minutes longer. Serve hot.

Pumpkin Custard

MAKES 4 SERVINGS

1 cup heavy cream
1 egg yolk and 2 whole eggs, lightly beaten
½ cup pumpkin puree, fresh or canned
2 tablespoons honey
1 tablespoon sugar
1 teaspoon ground cinnamon
Freshly grated nutmeg

1. Preheat the oven to 325° F. Butter four ½-cup custard cups (or any oven-proof dishes with a ½-cup capacity).

2. Heat the cream in a small, heavy saucepan. Remove from the heat and stir gradually into the beaten eggs. Stir in the pumpkin puree, honey, sugar, and cinnamon. Strain the mixture and divide it equally among the custard dishes. Grate nutmeg over each.

3. Place the custard dishes in a large baking dish or roasting pan. Fill the pan with enough boiling water to reach half-way up the sides of the custard dishes. Place the pan on a rack in the bottom third of the oven and bake until the custards are set, approximately 40 minutes. Cool before serving.

Ginger Cake

MAKES ONE 9-INCH CAKE

1⅓ cups sifted whole-wheat flour
1 cup all-purpose flour
¼ teaspoon salt
1 teaspoon baking powder
¼ teaspoon baking soda
1 teaspoon ground ginger
½ teaspoon ground mace
1 teaspoon ground cinnamon
½ teaspoon freshly grated nutmeg
½ teaspoon ground allspice
½ cup (1 stick) unsalted butter
1 cup dark brown sugar, tightly packed
2 eggs
½ cup molasses
¾ cup hot water

1. Preheat oven to 350° F. Generously butter one 9-inch square cake pan (or two 7-inch savarin molds, as we used).

2. Sift dry ingredients together and set aside.

3. Cream the butter and brown sugar until well blended and light. Beat in the eggs thoroughly; mix in the molasses. Add the flour mixture in small batches, alternating with the hot water. Blend well.

4. Pour the batter into the prepared pans and bake until a cake tester or toothpick inserted in the middle comes out clean, approximately 20 to 25 minutes. Let cool slightly in the pan, then turn out on cake rack to cool completely. Serve with pumpkin custard.

It is interesting to alter the flavor of a simple cup custard by adding a puree of butternut squash, carrot, or pumpkin —which tastes especially good with ginger cake.

Sautéed Duck Breasts

There are two basic kinds of duck available now in markets: the domestic Pekin and the darker, wilder-tasting Muscovy or mallard. The Pekin is white feathered, with light meat and tender skin; it is offered whole in supermarkets and butcher shops, The breast can be removed and the rest of the carcass used for a rich duck stock. Duck breasts from Muscovies and mallards are now offered at fancy groceries; they tend to be large and gamy and often have less fat than the Pekins. Whichever type I use, I like to steep the meat in a mild marinade of wine, oil, and juniper berries before cooking. The breasts can then be sautéed or grilled—but remember to render off the fat under the breast skin. The flatbread toasts can be arranged in advance, but don't heat them until right before serving so the melted cheese stays nice and soft.

I love this salad; the combination of the ultra-thin, tender beans with the apples and chèvre is so pretty, and so good. It is really the vegetable course for this meal, so make the individual servings generous.

While we were growing up, my mother was always inventing new and exciting desserts for her six children. This four-fruit milk sherbet was one of our favorites, and we all still make our own variations of it. My special contribution is to make it in heart-shaped ice cube trays—the presentation is really lovely.

This is a very autumnal menu—sautéed duck breasts and an apple-based salad—and I chose a setting of pale, fall colors: the yellow china, a pattern called Jasmine Golden Maire made in Sebring, Ohio, is set on an ivory damask table runner with ivory-handled flatware.

M E N U

SAUTÉED DUCK BREASTS
FLATBREAD WITH TOMATO PESTO
WAX BEAN, APPLE, AND CHÈVRE SALAD
FOUR-FRUIT SHERBET

Sautéed Duck Breasts

SERVES 4

2 whole duck breasts
2 tablespoons crushed juniper berries
¼ cup dry vermouth
2 tablespoons olive oil
2 cups duck stock or homemade Beef Stock (page 13)
1 tablespoon balsamic vinegar
12 medium spinach leaves

1. Place the duck breasts skins side down in a large baking dish.

2. Combine the juniper berries, vermouth, and oil and pour over the duck. Let marinate at room temperature for at least 30 minutes or overnight in the refrigerator. Remove from the marinade.

3. Heat a large cast-iron skillet over high heat until very hot—almost smoking. Add the duck breasts (one at a time if the pan is not large enough for both) skin side down and cook for 5 to 10 minutes to render the excess fat and brown the skin. Remove from the skillet and let drain on paper towels for several minutes.

4. Lower the heat to medium-high and sauté the duck breasts, beginning with the skin side, until rare, about 5 minutes on each side. Slice and keep warm.

5. In a small saucepan over high heat, reduce the stock to ½ cup. Remove from the heat and whisk in the vinegar.

6. Arrange slices of duck breast on the spinach and top with the warm sauce, which will wilt the leaves.

Flatbread with Tomato Pesto

SERVES 4

Sun-dried Tomato Pesto
8 whole sun-dried tomatoes
1 clove garlic
1 tablespoon pine nuts (pignoli)
½ cup fresh basil leaves
1 tablespoon fresh Parmesan cheese, grated
1 tablespoon fresh Romano cheese, grated
½ cup olive oil
Salt and freshly ground black pepper.

1 large, fresh flatbread
⅓ pound mozzarella cheese, grated

1. To make the tomato pesto, place the ingredients in a food processor and process until just blended.

2. Preheat the oven to 325° F.

3. Halve the flatbread and cut each half into 4 wedges. Slice horizontally through the middle of each wedge.

4. Spoon 1 teaspoon of pesto inside each wedge and cover the pesto with a little mozzarella. Bake until the cheese melts, 3 to 5 minutes, and serve immediately.

Wax Bean, Apple, and Chèvre Salad

SERVES 4

½ pound baby wax beans
½ red apple, cored and thinly sliced
½ green apple, cored and thinly sliced
1 head Belgian endive, leaves removed and quartered

8 small round (½-inch-thick) slices firm chèvre, preferably a combination of peppered and plain

Red Onion Vinaigrette
MAKES APPROXIMATELY ½ CUP
½ red onion, peeled and finely minced
3 tablespoons olive oil
1 tablespoon Champagne vinegar
Pinch of salt

1. Trim the ends of the baby wax beans and blanch them in a large pot of boiling water until tender, 3 to 4 minutes. Drain and plunge immediately into a container of ice water to stop any further cooking. Drain well.

2. Preheat the oven to 325° F.

3. Whisk together all ingredients for the vinaigrette and set aside.

4. In a large bowl combine the wax beans, apple slices, and endive. Toss gently with the vinaigrette. Divide the salad evenly among individual plates.

5. Warm rounds of goat cheese in the oven for 5 minutes. Place 2 rounds of cheese on each plate alongside the salad and serve.

Four-Fruit Sherbet

MAKES 1 GENEROUS QUART

1½ cups ripe strawberries, hulled
1 ripe banana, peeled and sliced
¼ cup lemon juice
¼ cup orange juice
1 teaspoon lemon zest
1 teaspoon orange zest
1½ cups sugar
4 cups cold milk

1. Place strawberries in a medium bowl along with the banana and fruit juices.

Using a fork or a potato masher, crush them together to make a coarse puree.

2. Stir in the zests, sugar, and milk; mix well.

3. Pour the mixture into ice cube trays (I used heart shapes) and freeze until firm. (The mixture can also be frozen in an ice-cream maker according to the manufacturer's directions.)

I froze this very simple four-fruit sherbet in heart-shape ice-cube trays; three or four hearts on a decorative glass plate make a generous and pretty serving.

Warm Mussel Salad

When I was still working on Wall Street, I discovered a terrific little Greenwich Village restaurant called La Petite Ferme. I loved the way they served mussels: cooked in their shells, dressed with a creamy mustard-shallot vinaigrette, and heaped to overflowing in great big wooden bowls. When we moved to Westport, I started making my own version of the dish, using fresh mussels from the beds in Long Island Sound. I like to hunt out the smaller mussels that cling together in great piles in rocky places—but large mussels are good, too. Whichever you use, they must be well scrubbed, with beards removed, and very clean.

I like to make this potato salad when new potatoes come in; it won't be very good if you use baking potatoes or "old" potatoes. And the warmer the potatoes are when sprinkled with vermouth, the more flavorful the salad will be.

The fennel bulbs will turn a golden brown when sautéed in hot olive oil, and their strong anise flavor will be mellowed. The sun-dried tomatoes are a really good addition; be sure to cut them into thin strips, as large chunks are just too strong-flavored to eat.

The chocolate mousse is rich and dense and simply wonderful in small quantities. I put it in dessert or parfait dishes before it sets so it looks perfect.

M E N U

Warm Mussel Salad
Sautéed Fennel
New Potatoes with Vermouth
Chocolate Mousse

Warm Mussel Salad

SERVES 4

6 *shallots, peeled and finely minced*
2 *tablespoons (¼ stick) unsalted butter*
1 *bottle dry white wine, preferably
    Sauvignon Blanc*
2 *quarts fresh mussels, well scrubbed
    and cleaned*

Dressing
MAKES 1½ CUPS
2 *tablespoons Dijon mustard*
¼ *cup white wine vinegar*
¾ *cup olive oil*
    Juice of ½ lemon
¼ *cup heavy cream*
½ *cup finely chopped fresh flat Italian
    parsley*
    Salt and freshly ground black pepper

1. In a large covered kettle, sauté the shallots in the butter until tender but not browned, about 5 minutes. Add the wine and bring to a boil.

2. Put the mussels in the kettle, cover, and return to a boil. Cook for 3 to 5 minutes, shaking the kettle every minute or so. Remove all open mussels at this point and continue to cook another minute or two until the remaining mussels have opened. (Discard any that have not yet opened.) Place the cooked mussels in a large serving bowl.

3. Combine all ingredients for the dressing and whisk until thick, creamy, and well blended. Drizzle the dressing over the hot mussels, toss to coat completely, and serve.

Sautéed Fennel

SERVES 4

6 *tablespoons olive oil*
4 *small bulbs fennel, sliced in thin
    strips*
4 *sun-dried tomatoes, cut into thin
    strips (optional)*
    Salt and freshly ground black pepper

Heat the oil in a large skillet until hot but not smoking. Add the fennel and stir over high heat until fennel turns gold, about 7 minutes. Stir in the sun-dried tomatoes, if desired, season lightly, and serve warm.

New Potatoes with Vermouth

SERVES 4

6 *long white-skinned new potatoes*
6 *tablespoons dry vermouth*
3 *tablespoons drained imported capers*
3 *teaspoons chopped fresh dill*

Dressing
MAKES 1 CUP
1½ *tablespoons Dijon mustard*
¾ *cup olive oil*
1½ *teaspoons white wine vinegar*
1½ *teaspoons fresh lemon juice*
    Salt and freshly ground white pepper

1. Gently simmer the potatoes in a pot of boiling water until tender, approximately 10 to 20 minutes. Do not let them get mushy. Drain well.

2. Whisk all dressing ingredients together until creamy. Set aside.

3. Cut the potatoes into ¼-inch slices and place in a large bowl. Drizzle with vermouth; add the capers, then the dressing. Toss gently to coat the potatoes, then top with dill. Serve immediately.

Chocolate Mousse

SERVES 4

6   ounces semisweet chocolate
½   cup (1 stick) unsalted butter
3   eggs, separated
2   tablespoons sugar
¾   cup heavy cream
½   teaspoon vanilla extract

1. In the top of a double boiler over simmering water, melt the chocolate with the butter. Transfer to a mixing bowl and set aside to cool.

2. When the chocolate mixture has reached room temperature, add the egg yolks and stir well.

3. Beat the egg whites to soft peaks, then, beating continuously, add the sugar. Whisk a small portion of egg white into the chocolate mixture to lighten it; gently fold in the remaining egg white.

4. Whip the cream with the vanilla until stiff, then fold it into the chocolate mixture carefully but thoroughly. Spoon the mixture into individual parfait dishes and chill until serving time.

I spooned the chocolate mousse into these green Depression glass cups before it set so it would look smooth and delicious; its color and texture are picked up by the silky damask tablecloth.

Whole Roasted Chicken with Goat Cheese and Sage

I can't remember when I first began inserting herbs and other flavorings under the skin of poultry, but it is a common practice in our kitchen nowadays. We stuff chicken breasts with ricotta and spinach or savory bread stuffings. Chickens of all sizes have their skins loosened, and herb leaves and spices are rubbed underneath. Sage, thyme, and rosemary can be inserted in decorative patterns for an unusual presentation. The method also works well with squab, turkey (page 176), and Cornish hens.

For this menu we insert rounds of goat cheese under the skin along with fresh sage leaves. The cavity of the bird is filled with more herbs; then the pan is strewn with onions, shallots, and garlic cloves to flavor the chicken even more during the roasting process. Basting the chicken and the vegetables with melted butter during their hour in the oven further enhances their taste and appearance.

The homemade pasta is flavored and colored with finely chopped flat-leaved parsley, and the sauce is a very simple combination of lightly sautéed fresh red peppers, garlic, and parsley leaves. Alongside the chicken and pasta we serve a mixture of colorful vegetables, which can be prepared, blanched, refreshed in ice water, and set aside while the chicken is roasting, then reheated while the poultry rests for a minute out of the oven.

This menu features strong, clear flavors, and it's best to end it with good, fresh fruit. When you find those perfect just ripe pears at the greengrocer's, try them plain with a wedge of fresh pecorino, a sharp and flavorful Italian hard cheese made from sheep's milk. (I like the Locatelli variety best.)

When Alexis got her first batch of Fiestaware from her great-grandmother, I found these striped runners, mats, and napkins for her. Their primary colors work well with the china and also pick up the bright reds, greens, and yellows of the vegetable mélange and the pasta with red pepper sauce.

M E N U

PARSLEY-FLECKED PASTA WITH RED PEPPER SAUCE
WHOLE ROASTED CHICKEN WITH GOAT CHEESE AND SAGE
COLORFUL MIXED VEGETABLES
PEARS AND PECORINO

Parsley-flecked Pasta with Red Pepper Sauce

SERVES 4 TO 6

Pasta
3½ cups all-purpose flour
⅓ cup finely chopped fresh parsley
1 teaspoon salt
5 eggs
1 tablespoon olive oil

Red Pepper Sauce
2 tablespoons (¼ stick) unsalted butter
3 tablespoons olive oil
4 cloves garlic, peeled and thinly sliced
2 large red bell peppers, seeded and cut into small triangles
1 cup whole fresh flat Italian parsley leaves
  Salt and freshly ground black pepper
  Pinch of cayenne pepper

Freshly grated Parmesan cheese

The chicken on its baking rack: see how the rounds of goat cheese and sage leaves make an attractive pattern beneath the skin of the breast and legs.

1. To make the pasta, combine the flour, parsley, and salt on a large board. Make a well in the center and break the eggs into it; add the olive oil. Gently mix all ingredients with a fork, then knead the dough with the heels of your hands until smooth, about 5 minutes. (If the dough seems sticky, add a little flour while kneading.)

2. Roll the dough out to the desired thickness with a pasta machine, following manufacturer's directions. Set the machine to fettuccine width and pass the noodles through it. Store well wrapped in freezer until ready to use.

3. To make the sauce, melt the butter and the olive oil in a skillet. Sauté the garlic until tender, about 5 minutes, but do not brown. Add the red peppers and sauté over medium heat for 5 minutes, tossing often, until the peppers have softened a bit. Remove from the heat and stir in the parsley, salt, pepper, and

cayenne. Set aside in a warm place.

4. Cook the pasta in a large pot of boiling water just until tender, approximately 2 to 4 minutes. Drain well.

5. Place the pasta on a serving platter and top with the hot red pepper sauce. Serve with Parmesan cheese.

Whole Roasted Chicken with Goat Cheese and Sage

SERVES 4

1 (3½-pound) roasting chicken
4 ounces goat cheese (a small log of Montrachet is perfect)
10 to 12 whole fresh sage leaves
1 bunch fresh herbs (such as flat Italian parsley, basil, chervil)
8 small white onions, peeled
8 shallots, peeled
4 cloves garlic, peeled
3 tablespoons unsalted butter, melted

1. Preheat the oven to 400° F.

2. With your fingers, gently loosen the skin of the chicken's breast and legs.

3. Cut the goat cheese into slices ¼ inch thick. Carefully place the rounds in a decorative pattern under the skin and press a sage leaf into each round.

4. Stuff the chicken with the fresh herbs and truss with butcher string. Place on a rack in a roasting pan and surround the chicken with the onions, shallots, and garlic. Roast, uncovered,

until the chicken is done, approximately 1 hour; baste occasionally with melted butter. Serve hot.

Colorful Mixed Vegetables

SERVES 4

¼ pound snow peas, stems and strings removed
2 carrots, peeled and thinly sliced
4 tiny white turnips, thinly sliced
2 tablespoons (¼ stick) unsalted butter
1 large red bell pepper, seeded and cut into strips
1 large yellow bell pepper, seeded and cut into strips
½ teaspoon fresh savory or thyme
Zest of 1 lemon
Salt and freshly ground black pepper

1. In a large pot of boiling water, blanch the snow peas until brightly colored and barely tender, about 1 minute. Blanch the carrots in the same water until brightly colored, about 3 to 4 minutes. Finally, blanch the turnips until barely tender, 3 to 4 minutes. Drain all the vegetables well and set aside.

2. In a large skillet, melt the butter and sauté the pepper strips for 3 minutes. Add the blanched vegetables, savory or thyme, and lemon zest and toss until warm. Season to taste and serve.

Pears and Pecorino

Pick out 1 ripe but firm, unblemished pear, preferably Bartlett, per person. Place on individual plates with a wedge of freshly cut pecorino cheese.

A beautiful pear—blush-skinned and ripe—with a wedge or two of cheese makes an excellent, simple dessert.

Roast Loin of Veal with Onion Preserves

This is a very elegant menu, perfect for a special occasion or a celebratory dinner with family or old friends. It may seem a little more complicated than most of the menus in this book, but everything really can be prepared in under an hour—and the result will be simply wonderful.

Loin of veal is rather expensive, but because the meat is rich and there is no waste whatever, a half pound of meat per serving will do nicely. Use the finest pale pink or white veal you can find; breast of veal can be substituted, but I much prefer the loin. This cut of meat comes from the butcher tied with string; using a butcher's steel, I make a hole lengthwise down the center of the loin and then fill it with the onion preserves, pushing them in with the handle of a wooden spoon. Take care to wrap the roast with parchment paper—it will help retain the juices.

Morels are elongated mushrooms with honeycomb-textured caps; they are usually darkish brown in color and have a woodland taste uniquely their own. Fresh morels are becoming available in the fall and winter—do try to find them.

The two purees can be made in advance and gently reheated. Notice that the turnip puree has a ripe pear in it; I often use a piece of fruit—an apple or a pear—to sweeten the vegetable. Even carrots sometimes need that additional flavor.

The dessert is a French classic called *oeufs à la neige*, or *îles flottantes*—floating islands. It is simply stiffly whipped egg whites gently poached in sweetened milk or water and served on a pool of crème Anglaise, but it looks very impressive and tastes—especially when flavored with hazelnut liqueur—delicious.

A wonderful, warm-toned meal for a late November day—roast loin of veal with purees of carrot and white turnip set on Cameo-pattern amber Depression glass borrowed from my friend Aimee. The tablecloth is a shiny damask; the flowers are amber and yellow freesia and ranunculuses.

MENU

SAUTÉED MORELS
ROAST LOIN OF VEAL WITH ONION PRESERVES
CARROT PUREE
PUREE OF WHITE TURNIP
OEUFS À LA NEIGE WITH HAZELNUT CRÈME ANGLAISE

Sautéed Morels

SERVES 4 TO 6

3 tablespoons unsalted butter
¼ pound fresh morels, or 2 ounces dried
1 tablespoon chopped fresh flat Italian parsley
Salt and freshly ground black pepper

1. If using dried morels, soak in ½ cup warm water for 20 minutes; drain well.

2. Melt the butter in a large skillet. Sauté morels for 3 minutes. Sprinkle with parsley and season to taste. Serve immediately.

Roast Loin of Veal
with Onion Preserves

SERVES 4 TO 6

Onion Preserves
2 *tablespoons (¼ stick) unsalted butter*
3 *tablespoons olive oil*
2 *onions, peeled, halved, and thinly sliced lengthwise*
4 *teaspoons dark brown sugar*
⅛ *teaspoon balsamic vinegar*
⅓ *cup dry red wine*
  Salt and freshly ground black pepper

3 *pounds boneless loin of veal, tied at 1½-inch intervals*
3 *large onions, peeled and minced*
2 *cloves garlic, peeled and minced*
  Salt and freshly ground black pepper

1. To make the onion preserves, heat the butter and oil in a heavy, medium skillet and cook the onions over low heat until softened but not browned, approximately 20 minutes. Sprinkle with the brown sugar, and over low heat, cook until evenly browned. Stir in the vinegar and wine and simmer until the liquids are completely absorbed. Season to taste.

2. Preheat the oven to 400° F.

3. Using a butcher's steel, make a hole down the center of the veal loin. Fill with onion preserves, stuffing them in with the handle of a wooden spoon.

4. Place the veal on a large sheet of parchment paper and sprinkle the minced onions and garlic around and over the meat. Season to taste and roll up the meat in the parchment, twisting the ends closed. (This will keep the meat very moist while cooking.) Place the meat in a roasting pan or shallow baking dish and roast for 45 to 60 minutes. The minced onions should be cooked almost to a puree and the meat should be tender when pierced with a fork. Remove the parchment paper and let the veal rest 10 minutes out of the oven before slicing.

Carrot Puree

SERVES 4 TO 6

1½ *pounds carrots, peeled and cut into 2-inch pieces*
4 *tablespoons (½ stick) unsalted butter*
1 *teaspoon sugar*
  Salt and freshly ground black pepper
  Freshly grated nutmeg
  Pinch of fresh thyme

1. Put the carrots into a heavy saucepan, barely cover with water, and add butter and sugar. Cook over medium heat until very tender, approximately 20 to 30 minutes.

2. Drain the carrots and puree them in a blender or food processor until smooth. Season with salt, pepper, nutmeg, and thyme. Serve hot.

Puree of White Turnip

SERVES 4 TO 6

8 *white turnips, peeled and quartered*
1 *ripe pear, peeled, cored, and chopped*
2 *tablespoons (¼ stick) unsalted butter*
  Salt and freshly ground black pepper

1. Place the turnips in a heavy saucepan and cover with water. Cook over medium heat until tender, approximately 15 to 20 minutes.

2. Drain the turnips and place in the bowl of a food processor with the pear and butter. Puree until smooth and season to taste. Serve hot.

NOTE: Purees can be prepared ahead of time and reheated over a pot of simmering water before serving. If purees are too thick, add a bit of cream to thin the mixture slightly.

Oeufs à la Neige with Hazelnut Crème Anglaise

SERVES 4 TO 6

Hazelnut Crème Anglaise
2½ cups milk
 ¼ cup sugar
  3 egg yolks, beaten
  1 tablespoon Frangelico (hazelnut liqueur)

Meringues
  4 egg whites
 ⅓ teaspoon cream of tartar
  7 tablespoons sugar
 ½ teaspoon vanilla extract
     Milk for poaching

Caramel
 ¼ cup sugar
  2 tablespoons water

1. To make the crème Anglaise, combine the milk and sugar in a saucepan and heat until the sugar dissolves. Place the beaten egg yolks in a bowl and gradually add the hot sweetened milk, whisking constantly. Put the mixture in a clean saucepan and cook over low heat, stirring constantly, until the mixture coats a wooden spoon, about 10 minutes. Remove from the heat, stir in the liqueur, and chill thoroughly.

2. Place the egg whites in the top of a double boiler over warm water until just tepid. Remove from the heat and beat at high speed with the cream of tartar until stiff but not dry. Beat in the sugar and vanilla; do not overbeat the meringue.

3. Fill a large skillet with milk and bring to a boil. Reduce the heat to a simmer; the milk temperature should not go above 170° F.

4. Place the meringue mixture in a pastry bag fitted with a large star tip. Pipe as many large pyramids of meringue into the milk as possible; cover and poach for 8 minutes. Carefully remove the meringues with a slotted spoon and let cool, draining on paper towels. Repeat until all the meringue mixture is used.

5. Arrange the cooled meringues on a pool of crème Anglaise.

6. To make the caramel, swirl (do not stir) the sugar and water together in a heavy saucepan and cook over high heat until it caramelizes. Remove from the heat and let cool a few moments. Using a fork, drizzle the tops of the meringues with the warm caramel.

Shallow amber bowls are perfect for the oeufs à la neige, which are served floating in a soup of crème Anglaise. A bit of amber caramel is swirled over the top of each meringue.

Seafood Risotto

We conduct monthly entertaining seminars in Westport and often prepare an antipasto buffet for demonstration. One of the most popular dishes we serve, along with the finger foods, is this seafood risotto. We use Italian short-grain rice and cook it with a light chicken stock until it is creamy. The various seafoods are marinated in fresh citrus juices, then lightly sautéed and added to the fully cooked rice. A perfect risotto should be creamy, never sticky, and the rice should be tender and chewy.

The string beans we used, French haricots verts, are very thin, tender beans with a lovely dark green color. They are becoming increasingly popular and are available most of the year. They combine well in this recipe with the baby carrots and the sautéed radicchio; fresh rosemary adds an unusual flavor.

The salad is a bit Italian in feeling and uses both bitter dandelion and pungent arugula. Bibb lettuce and mild chervil leaves lighten up the mixture.

During the winter months, a very special orange—the blood orange—is available in some markets. I have used these oranges not only for juice but also sectioned in desserts, salads, and on fruit platters. They always provoke comment. Here I peeled them and sliced them crosswise, then placed them on dessert plates with slices of regular navel oranges so the color contrast would be very evident.

Whenever I spot an unusual piece of cloth at a tag sale or house sale, I buy it to make into a pillowcase, a table covering, or even to cut up into napkins. This piece of cotton is probably American; its blue and orange Tattersall check is the perfect background for the orange Fiestaware plates, which in turn are the right setting for this seafood risotto.

MENU

SEAFOOD RISOTTO
SALAD OF DANDELION, ARUGULA, AND BIBB LETTUCE
BABY STRING BEANS, TINY CARROTS, AND RADICCHIO
BLOOD ORANGES WITH GRAND MARNIER

Seafood Risotto

SERVES 8

Juice of 1 orange
¾ pound bay scallops
Juice of ½ grapefruit
¾ pound medium shrimp, peeled and deveined
½ cup (1 stick) unsalted butter
⅓ cup finely minced shallots
2 cups Arborio rice
4 cups Chicken Stock (page 13), heated to boiling
Large pinch of saffron threads
¼ cup olive oil
¼ pound small shiitake or brown Italian mushrooms, trimmed and tops scored
½ cup freshly grated Parmesan cheese
Salt and freshly ground black pepper
2 tablespoons chopped fresh flat Italian parsley
8 large Mediterranean shrimp or South African scampi (optional)

1. Pour the orange juice over the scallops and let marinate for 30 minutes. Pour the grapefruit juice over the shrimp and let marinate for 30 minutes.

2. Melt the butter in a heavy 4-quart saucepan and sauté the shallots until they are tender but not browned, about 5 minutes.

3. Add the rice and sauté until it turns opaque.

4. Add ½ cup of the boiling stock and the saffron to the saucepan and cook over medium heat, stirring constantly, until all liquid is absorbed. Immediately add ½ cup more boiling stock, stirring constantly. Continue in this manner until all stock is used and the rice is tender but still a bit firm. The rice should be cooked, and all the liquid absorbed, in 18 to 20 minutes. Remove from the heat and keep in a warm place.

5. Heat one-third of the oil in a skillet and sauté the scallops for 2 to 3 minutes. Remove the scallops with a slotted spoon and stir into the risotto.

6. Heat half the remaining oil in the same skillet and sauté the shrimp just until they turn pink, 2 to 3 minutes. Stir gently into the risotto.

7. Heat the remaining oil in the same skillet and sauté the mushrooms just until softened, 5 minutes. Stir into the risotto.

8. Return the risotto to a low heat and stir in the Parmesan cheese. Season to taste and sprinkle with the parsley. Serve immediately, garnished with the large shrimp, if available.

Salad of Dandelion, Arugula, and Bibb Lettuce

SERVES 8

1 large handful of a combination of dandelion greens, arugula, and bibb lettuce per person

Dressing
MAKES ¾ CUP
½ cup olive oil
¼ cup balsamic vinegar
2 tablespoons Dijon mustard
Salt and freshly ground black pepper

Combine salad greens in a large bowl. Whisk the dressing ingredients together and toss with salad right before serving.

Baby String Beans, Tiny Carrots, and Radicchio

SERVES 8

¾ pound tiny carrots, peeled and julienned
1 pound small string beans, stem ends removed
3 tablespoons unsalted butter
2 heads radicchio, shredded coarsely
 Salt and freshly ground black pepper
1 pinch fresh rosemary leaves (optional)

1. In a large pot of boiling water, blanch the carrots until tender, 3 minutes. Remove with a slotted spoon and drain.

2. In the same pot, bring water back to a boil and blanch the string beans until tender, 3 to 5 minutes. Remove from heat and drain.

3. Melt the butter in a large skillet and sauté the radicchio for 1 minute. Sprinkle with salt and pepper to taste and add the carrots, string beans, and, if desired, rosemary. Toss well and serve.

Blood Oranges with Grand Marnier

SERVES 8

8 small blood oranges
3 large navel oranges
½ cup Grand Marnier
 Fresh fruit-scented mint leaves, preferably dark-purple grapefruit mint

1. With a sharp paring knife, cut the peel from all the oranges, removing all the white pith yet cutting as little of the pulp as possible. Slice each orange crosswise into ¼-inch slices.

2. Arrange the blood orange slices and several navel orange slices on individual serving plates. Sprinkle each with a tablespoon of Grand Marnier and chill until ready to serve, garnished with leaves of grapefruit mint.

Roasted Turkey Breast

Strictly speaking, this is not a Quick Cook menu; if you have a 5-pound turkey breast, it may need to roast for up to 1½ hours, longer than our goal of meal preparation in under one hour. But it is so easy to prepare and leaves you with such wonderful leftovers, I'm including it anyway.

Turkey breasts can be found fresh or frozen; I prefer to use the fresh ones—I think they are usually juicier and tastier. I loosen the skin from the breast and rub the meat with an herb dressing; by inserting parsley leaves or some other herbs under the skin, you can make a decorative pattern that shows up after roasting—and make the turkey much more flavorful.

Popovers are loved by everyone. I've learned always to make more than I think I'll need, and even so, there are never any left over. They must be eaten right out of the oven; serve them with butter and gravy, jam, or conserve.

The cold lemon soufflé can be served from one large bowl or from individual dessert cups or goblets—just remember it will look prettier if you spoon it into its serving dish before it sets. This same mixture, by the way, makes wonderful lemon tarts or tartlets, especially with a garnish of mint leaves, lemon slices, or edible blossoms.

M E N U

ROASTED TURKEY BREAST
POPOVERS
ASPARAGUS WITH GREEN HERB HOLLANDAISE
MANDARIN ORANGE AND PECAN SALAD
COLD LEMON SOUFFLÉ

Roasted Turkey Breast

SERVES 6

Herb Dressing
 ¼ cup light olive oil
 3 tablespoons chopped fresh flat Italian
 parsley
 1 teaspoon fresh thyme leaves
 1 teaspoon fresh marjoram leaves
 ½ teaspoon lemon zest
 ¼ teaspoon salt
 ⅛ teaspoon freshly ground black pepper

 1 (4- to 5-pound) turkey breast, fresh
 or frozen and thawed
 1 small bunch flat Italian parsley,
 stems removed

1. Preheat the oven to 350° F.

2. Quickly whisk together the herb
dressing ingredients until well blended.

3. Rinse the turkey breast and pat dry
with a paper towel. Using your fingers,
gently separate the skin from the breast
meat and arrange the parsley leaves dec-
oratively on top of the meat. Pour about
2 tablespoons of the herb dressing
evenly over the breast meat and parsley
leaves and stretch the skin back over the
meat. Pin the skin around the sides of
the breast with small wooden skewers
to prevent it from shrinking.

4. Brush the remaining dressing over
the entire breast with a pastry brush.

5. Roast the turkey until the juices run
clear, 1 to 1½ hours (180° F on a meat
thermometer). Let sit at least 15 minutes before carving and serving.

Popovers

MAKES 10 LARGE POPOVERS

 2 tablespoons (¼ stick) unsalted
 butter, melted
 2 cups milk
 2 cups all-purpose flour, sifted
 1 teaspoon salt
 4 eggs, lightly beaten

1. Preheat the oven to 450° F. Butter
and lightly flour 10 muffin cups, pop-
over tins, or custard dishes. Set aside.

2. Whisk together the butter, milk,
flour, and salt until smooth. Whisk in
the beaten eggs, a bit at a time, until
incorporated. Do not overbeat the batter; it should have the consistency of
heavy cream.

3. Fill the prepared dishes three-
fourths full with the batter. Bake 15
minutes.

4. Without opening the oven, lower the
heat to 350° F. and bake popovers 15
to 20 minutes longer. Serve hot.

Asparagus with Green Herb Hollandaise

SERVES 6

 1 pound green asparagus
 ¾ pound white asparagus

Green Herb Hollandaise
 3 egg yolks, lightly beaten
 1 to 2 tablespoons fresh lemon juice, or
 to taste
 ¼ teaspoon salt
 Pinch of freshly ground white pepper
 1 tablespoon chopped fresh flat Italian
 parsley
 1 tablespoon chopped fresh dill
 ½ cup (1 stick) unsalted butter, melted
 until foamy

1. Trim the asparagus so that they are all the same length. Remove any tough outer skin with a vegetable peeler.

2. Blanch the asparagus in a large pot of boiling water until just tender, 4 to 5 minutes. Drain well and keep warm while preparing the sauce.

3. To make the hollandaise, combine all ingredients except the butter in a blender jar and mix well. With the motor running at high speed, add the hot butter, a drop at a time, until the mixture is smooth and thoroughly blended.

4. Place the asparagus on a serving platter and top with the hollandaise. Serve immediately.

Mandarin Orange and Pecan Salad

SERVES 6

1 handful of a combination of curly chicory and green leaf lettuce per person
1 (11-ounce) can mandarin oranges, drained
½ cup toasted pecan halves

Dressing
MAKES APPROXIMATELY ½ CUP
1 small shallot, peeled and chopped
¼ cup balsamic vinegar
Salt and freshly ground black pepper
3 tablespoons light olive oil
1 tablespoon walnut oil

Place the lettuces in a large serving bowl. Whisk all dressing ingredients together in a small bowl. Right before serving, toss the lettuce with the dressing. Top with the orange segments and pecans.

Cold Lemon Soufflé

MAKES 2 QUARTS

¾ cup sugar
⅓ cup lemon juice
1 package unflavored gelatin, softened in 1 tablespoon water
6 egg whites
¾ cup heavy cream, stiffly whipped
Grated zest of 1 lemon
Fresh mint leaves, candied lemon peel, or lemon slices (optional)

1. In a small saucepan over low heat, dissolve the sugar in the lemon juice. Add the softened gelatin and cook until mixture is smooth and gelatin is dissolved. Cool the mixture over ice water until slightly thickened but not set.

2. Whip the egg whites until stiff. Beat in the lemon mixture. Gently fold in the whipped cream and lemon zest.

3. Spoon the mixture into individual serving dishes or a large bowl. Refrigerate for at least 1 hour before serving. If desired, garnish with mint leaves, candied peel, or paper-thin slices of lemon.

The lemon soufflé is served cold, spooned from a pressed glass bowl onto individual dessert plates, with paper-thin lemon slices as a garnish.

Pork Chops with Soy-Orange Sauce

For this homey meal of pork chops and green cabbage with rice, I chose outsized white plates from Jackson Custom China, flatware (also outsized) from Christophle, and cobalt-blue glasses with red and blue plaid linen mats and napkins that were handwoven in the 1880s from homespun flax.

Ever since I was a child, I have loved pork chops. Even now, when I am trying not to eat much meat, I will buy very thin pork chops and cook them with soy sauce, orange juice, and garlic. They are especially good if quickly browned and served with sautéed thyme sprigs. (Sautéed herbs are crispy and delicious—try rosemary, sage, and even parsley and chervil.)

The green cabbage with rice is a comforting kind of dish, very easy to make and perfect with the pork chops. I like the texture and taste of Japanese rice here—my favorite brand is called Kokohu Rose.

With their bittersweet flavor, blood oranges taste very good in salads. Here I combined them with red oakleaf lettuce and radicchio to make a very interesting combination of flavors—and colors.

If you can possibly locate Golden Criterions for the dessert, do so. These sweet apples bake beautifully, and the skin becomes as tender as the flesh. The lemon zest, butter, and sugar are all you need for flavoring.

M E N U

GREEN CABBAGE WITH RICE
PORK CHOPS WITH SOY-ORANGE SAUCE
RADICCHIO AND BLOOD ORANGE SALAD
BAKED APPLES

Green Cabbage with Rice

SERVES 4

- 2 tablespoons vegetable oil
- 1½ cups white rice, preferably short-grain oriental rice
- 3 cups boiling Chicken Stock (page 13) or water
  Salt and freshly ground black pepper
- 2 bay leaves
- 2 sprigs fresh flat Italian parsley
- ½ pound green cabbage, coarsely chopped
- 3 tablespoons olive oil

1. In a heavy, 2-quart covered casserole, heat the vegetable oil until hot. Add the rice and sauté until it becomes opaque, 3 to 4 minutes.

2. Heat stock or water to boiling and pour over the rice. Add bay leaves and parsley and season to taste. Reduce heat, cover, and cook until all the liquid has been absorbed and the rice is tender, approximately 20 minutes. Remove from heat and keep warm.

3. In a large, heavy skillet, sauté the cabbage in olive oil until tender and bright green, about 4 minutes. Season to taste.

4. Stir the cabbage into the rice and serve hot.

The dark reds of the radicchio and blood orange salad contrast well with the cobalt blue of the Depression glass plate.

Opposite: *Apples baked with lemon zest not only taste wonderful, they fill the house with their scent while they cook.*

Pork Chops with Soy-Orange Sauce

SERVES 4

¾ cup fresh orange juice
2 tablespoons soy sauce
1 teaspoon sugar
1 clove garlic, peeled and crushed
¼ teaspoon freshly ground black pepper
8 sprigs fresh thyme

2 tablespoons (¼ stick) butter
2 tablespoons safflower oil
8 lean (½-inch-thick) loin pork chops

1. Combine orange juice with the soy sauce, sugar, garlic, pepper, and thyme sprigs. Set aside.

2. With a very sharp knife, score the pork chops ⅛ inch deep in a crisscross pattern on each side. Place in a glass or stainless steel dish in a single layer. Pour the marinade over chops and let sit at least 30 minutes. Drain and reserve the marinade.

3. Heat the butter and oil in a large, heavy skillet until hot. Add the chops in a single layer and sauté over high heat for 3 minutes on each side, browning them well.

4. Reduce heat to low and pour reserved marinade over chops. Cook until done, about 8 to 10 minutes longer. Remove chops to a heated platter.

5. Reduce the marinade in the skillet to ⅓ cup. Pour over the cooked chops and serve immediately.

NOTE: These pork chops are also excellent grilled over hot coals. Reduce the marinade separately in a saucepan and pour over the chops after removing from grill.

Radicchio and Blood Orange Salad

SERVES 4

1 handful red oakleaf lettuce per person
1 blood orange, sectioned, with membranes removed
1 head radicchio, shredded
2 scallions, trimmed and sliced diagonally

Dressing
MAKES ½ CUP
¼ cup sunflower oil
2 tablespoons olive oil
1 teaspoon Dijon mustard
1 tablespoon fresh orange juice
Salt and freshly ground black pepper

Combine the lettuce, orange sections, radicchio, and scallions in a large salad bowl. Whisk the dressing ingredients together and pour over the salad greens. Toss gently and serve immediately on individual salad plates.

Baked Apples

SERVES 4

4 Golden Criterion or Rome Beauty apples, whole, unpeeled, and cored
¼ cup plus 1 tablespoon sugar
Zest of 4 lemons
4 tablespoons (½ stick) unsalted butter, melted

1. Preheat the oven to 375° F.

2. Butter a baking dish large enough to hold the apples, then set them in.

3. Combine the sugar and lemon zest. Fill each apple core with a portion. Drizzle the butter over the tops and bake until tender, approximately 20 minutes.

Oriental Five-Spice Hens

This menu was inspired by my love of Oriental cuisine—and provides another example of how easy it is to produce wonderful Oriental meals at home if one has just the right ingredients. The Chinese-style dumplings are made from scratch: the dough is a simple flour and water mixture that is kneaded and rolled very thin. One can substitute wonton wrappers or dumpling skins that can be purchased in Asian markets. For the filling, I used our own smoked chicken, but, again, store-bought smoked chicken could be used. (While I boiled these dumplings, they can also be fried—in which case they are called *potstickers*.)

The five-spice hens are partially boned, highly seasoned inside and out, reconstructed, and roasted with a glaze of guava jelly and spices. The fresh ginger, coriander, red pepper flakes, and orange zest make these hens very special; they are good right out of the oven but also make a terrific picnic entrée served at room temperature or cold. The curried couscous, on the other hand, is best eaten shortly after it has been prepared.

While we were readying this menu for photography, I found these baby cauliflowers. They were at the greengrocer's for only one or two weeks, but because the taste of these miniatures is wonderfully accurate (sometimes miniature vegetables have less flavor than the full-size variety), I do hope we'll see more of them. They were so perfect, all I had to do was blanch the heads entire and serve them hot with the pan juices from the hens.

The plum ice should be made from a red, ripe plum: try to pick a sweet fruit like a Santa Rosa or Santa Clara. Served with canned or fresh peeled litchis, it is the perfect Oriental dessert.

I love Oriental food and have adapted several dishes to Quick Cook standards: the five-spice hen (served on a luster-edge plate) and Chinese dumplings (on a silver luster plate) are simple to prepare, and both look and taste quite exotic.

MENU

CHINESE DUMPLINGS
ORIENTAL FIVE-SPICE HENS
CURRIED COUSCOUS
BABY CAULIFLOWER
PLUM ICE WITH LITCHIS

It takes a bit of practice, but the boning of a Cornish hen is not too difficult. Marinating the meat with spices and herbs enhances the flavor immensely.

Chinese Dumplings

MAKES APPROXIMATELY 12

Dipping Sauce
- 2 tablespoons soy sauce
- 2 tablespoons rice wine vinegar
- 1 teaspoon finely chopped scallions

Dumplings
- ¾ cup all-purpose flour
- ¼ cup water
- ¼ to ½ cup finely shredded smoked duck or chicken breast
  Several leaves of fresh spinach, washed and dried, torn in pieces
- 1 egg white

1. To make the dipping sauce, combine all ingredients and set aside.

2. In a bowl, mix the flour and water with a fork until thoroughly blended and smooth. Remove from the bowl and knead on a lightly floured surface for 3 to 5 minutes. Let rest, covered, for 30 minutes.

3. Roll the dough into an even cylinder approximately 1 inch in diameter. Cut into slices ⅛ inch thick and roll each slice into a 4-inch round. (Trim with a fluted biscuit cutter, if desired.) Place approximately ½ tablespoon of duck or chicken meat and a small piece of spinach on half of each round; fold over and seal with a bit of egg white. Press the edges securely.

4. Cook the dumplings in a pot of boiling water for 3 to 4 minutes. Drain well.

5. Serve hot or warm with dipping sauce.

Oriental Five-Spice Hens

SERVES 2

- 2 small Cornish hens
- 1 (1-inch) piece fresh ginger, slivered and mashed
- 1 teaspoon five-spice powder
- 1 teaspoon salt
- 1 tablespoon oriental sesame oil
- ½ teaspoon red pepper flakes
- 1 teaspoon orange zest
- 6 sprigs fresh coriander (cilantro)
- ¼ cup sliced scallions (white and green parts)
- 2 tablespoons guava jelly

1. Remove the backbones, breastbones, and ribs of the hens by placing each on a board, breast side down. Cut along both sides of the backbone with a very sharp knife. Cut the meat from the rib cage, keeping the knife as close to the bone as possible. Pull the entire carcass from the meat. Cut out the thigh bones.

2. With the hens skin side down, rub the ginger onto the meat of each hen and leave several slivers on each.

3. Combine the five-spice powder, salt, sesame oil, red pepper flakes, and orange zest and sprinkle ½ teaspoon of this mixture over each hen. Place 2 to 3 sprigs of coriander on each hen and sprinkle with the scallions.

4. "Sew" the backs of each hen with a bamboo skewer, completely enclosing the ginger, spice mixture, coriander, and scallions inside, and truss with kitchen string. Let rest at room temperature for at least 10 minutes.

5. Preheat the oven to 350° F.

6. Add the guava jelly to the remaining five-spice marinade and heat gently to melt the jelly.

7. Place the hens in a baking dish and baste with the guava glaze. Bake until done, approximately 45 minutes.

Curried Couscous

SERVES 2

1 tablespoon olive oil
1 shallot, finely minced
¼ cup finely chopped scallions
1 cup quick-cooking couscous
1 cup hot Chicken Stock (page 13)
1 teaspoon soy sauce
2 teaspoons unsalted butter
1 tablespoon curry powder
½ teaspoon sugar
   Salt and freshly ground black pepper

1. In a medium-size, heavy saucepan, heat the olive oil. Add the shallot and scallions and cook until soft but not browned, 3 minutes. Add the couscous and sauté 1 to 2 minutes more.

2. In a separate saucepan, combine the remaining ingredients and bring to a boil. Pour immediately over the sautéed couscous, remove from the heat, and let stand until the liquid has been absorbed and couscous is tender, 10 to 15 minutes. Serve hot.

Baby Cauliflower

SERVES 2

2 or 3 heads tiny cauliflower, untrimmed

1. In a large pot of boiling water, blanch the cauliflower just until tender, approximately 5 to 7 minutes. Drain well.

2. To serve, glaze the blanched cauliflower with drippings from the Cornish hens roasting pan.

Plum Ice with Litchis

MAKES 1 PINT

8 ripe red plums
2 ripe black plums
2 tablespoons sweet Japanese plum wine
¼ cup sugar, approximately
   Fresh or canned litchis

1. Blanch the plums in a large pot of boiling water for no more than 1 minute. Remove with a slotted spoon and immediately peel off the skins.

2. When the plums are cool enough to handle, remove the pits and puree the fruit. Strain them twice to remove the fibers by putting them through a medium sieve first, then a fine-mesh sieve.

3. Pour the plum mixture into a small saucepan, stir in the plum wine, and add sugar to taste. Heat just until the sugar dissolves. Remove from the heat and chill thoroughly.

4. Freeze the plum mixture in an ice-cream maker according to the manufacturer's directions.

5. Serve with fresh or canned litchis.

Litchi fruits are served with same-size scoops of plum ice in a cut-glass goblet.

Oyster Stew

Once while on an assignment for the *New York Times*, I met a caterer named Dorothy Brummel. She and her daughter lived on the Chesapeake Bay where they specialized in cooking oysters. Their oyster stew was buttery and rich, with large, plump, barely coddled oysters floating in it. This recipe is an adaptation of Dorothy's and can be made with Long Island Sound oysters, as it is here, or with any other variety. Just insist on the very sweetest, freshest oysters, as Dorothy does.

I often make buttermilk biscuits on Sunday morning to serve with poached eggs and grits; any leftovers are frozen, well wrapped. They reheat very well and represent another way to make even the simplest meal appear more elaborate.

The stuffed artichokes are very easy to make. Choose large, firm, unblemished artichokes, trim them well, and cook them long enough so that they are really tender. The filling is made from spaghetti squash: when baked for 45 minutes or so, the flesh of this squash can be removed in long, spaghettilike tendrils that taste quite wonderful flavored with just butter, scallions, and thyme.

For dessert—baked bananas. Use ripe, sweet bananas; underripe fruit tends to be a bit starchy and bitter. We used cardamom as a flavoring; you could also sprinkle some rum over the fruit while it is baking.

MENU

OYSTER STEW
BUTTERMILK BISCUITS
STUFFED ARTICHOKES
BAKED BANANAS WITH CREAM

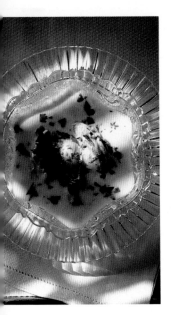

Oyster stew with a sprinkling of parsley looks simply delicious in a pressed glass plate.

Preceding page: When I'm home alone I like to eat dinner in bed, curled up with a good book or even with the TV on (if there's a good movie showing). This meal of oyster stew and stuffed artichokes is perfect bedroom fare, especially when served on a large tray—big enough to accommodate an entire dinner and keep crumbs out of the sheets.

Oyster Stew

SERVES 4

   4 tablespoons (½ stick) unsalted butter
   1 quart shucked oysters, drained, their
       liquor reserved and strained
   2 cups heavy cream
   2 cups milk
       Salt and freshly ground black pepper
   ¼ cup chopped fresh flat Italian parsley

1. In a large skillet, melt the butter. When it begins to bubble, add the oysters and heat for 2 or 3 minutes.

2. Combine the cream, milk, and strained oyster liquor in a large saucepan. Heat thoroughly and add the oysters; heat the mixture through again but do not allow it to boil.

3. Season the oyster stew to taste and sprinkle with chopped parsley. Serve immediately.

Buttermilk Biscuits

MAKES APPROXIMATELY 10 BISCUITS

1½ cups all-purpose flour
   1 tablespoon baking powder
   ¼ teaspoon baking soda
   1 tablespoon sugar
   ½ teaspoon salt
   ½ cup solid vegetable shortening, or a
       combination of shortening and butter
   ¼ to ⅓ cup buttermilk
   1 tablespoon heavy cream

1. Preheat the oven to 400° F. Line a large baking sheet with parchment paper.

2. Sift the dry ingredients together into a large bowl. Cut in the shortening until the mixture resembles rolled oats. Cover and refrigerate for at least 20 minutes.

3. Make a well in the center of the mixture and add just enough buttermilk to hold it together. Stir quickly with your fingers until just combined. (It doesn't matter if some flour is left in the bowl.)

4. Turn the mixture out onto a lightly floured board and roll into a ¾-inch-thick rectangle. Cut as many biscuits as possible from the dough with a 2½-inch biscuit cutter and place on the baking sheet, leaving a little space between for expansion.

5. Brush the tops of the biscuits with the cream and bake until lightly golden, 13 to 15 minutes. Let cool on racks.

Stuffed Artichokes

SERVES 4

   ½ medium spaghetti squash, cut
       lengthwise
   4 artichokes
   ¼ cup olive oil
   4 cloves garlic, peeled
       Juice of ¼ lemon
       Salt and freshly ground black pepper
   2 scallions, green and white parts sliced
   2 tablespoons (¼ stick) unsalted butter
   1 teaspoon fresh thyme leaves

1. Preheat the oven to 350° F.

2. Place the spaghetti squash cut side down in a shallow baking dish. Add ¼ inch water and bake until the squash is barely squeezable and the flesh is tender, 40 to 45 minutes. Let cool before scraping out the spaghetti-like strings of flesh with a fork or spoon.

3. While the squash bakes, prepare the artichokes by cutting off the stems and pointed tops and scissoring off the prickly points of the leaves. Set in a pot large enough to hold them and add water to cover three-fourths of the artichokes. Drizzle with the olive oil.

4. Add the garlic, lemon juice, and salt and pepper to the pot and bring to a boil. Cover and cook the artichokes for 30 minutes. Remove from the pot and let cool slightly before prying the centers of the artichokes apart and scooping out the hairy chokes with a sharp spoon.

5. To make the filling, sauté the scallions in the butter until softened, approximately 3 minutes. Add the spaghetti squash and thyme and season to taste; heat through.

6. To serve, fill the cavity of each artichoke with a portion of the filling, mounding it a bit over the top.

Baked Bananas with Cream

SERVES 4

4 firm bananas
6 tablespoons dark brown sugar
¼ cup (½ stick) unsalted butter
6 cardamom seed pods, husks removed and black seeds crushed
½ cup heavy cream

1. Preheat the oven to 450° F. Butter a large baking dish and set aside.

2. Peel and cut the bananas diagonally into ⅜-inch slices.

3. Place the banana slices in the prepared baking dish and sprinkle with 2 tablespoons of the brown sugar. Bake 5 minutes.

4. Remove the bananas from the oven, immediately sprinkle with the remaining brown sugar, and dot with butter.

5. Divide the banana slices equally among individual dessert plates and sprinkle with the cardamom. Pour a bit of cream around the slices and serve immediately.

Bananas baked with brown sugar, butter, and cream —a simple dessert on a simple setting, a Sandwich glass plate and a hemstitched, waffleweave napkin.

Fettuccine with Pumpkin-Cream Sauce

At Harry's Bar in Venice, the carpaccio is served on large white platters, the tissue-thin slices of raw beef drizzled with a garlic-scented mayonnaise until they look like white-veined red marble. I like to serve the meat with a garnish of thin curls of Parmesan cheese, leaves of red lettuce or arugula, and a sprinkling of fresh lemon juice. A small serving will suffice for an appetizer, and a large plate can be a main course for lunch or dinner.

The fresh, sweet pumpkin sauce for the fettuccine combines cream, egg yolks, and pumpkin puree. (If you don't have fresh sugar pumpkin, use frozen pumpkin puree—the canned pumpkin does not have such sweet flavor.) The pasta can be fresh, store-bought fettuccine—or, of course, you can make your own egg-pasta fettuccine. As a topping for the fettuccine or as a side dish, sauté some fennel, pumpkin strips, and prosciutto.

This coffee sherbet made from very strong espresso goes wonderfully with amaretti—Italian almond macaroons—on the side. And if, after dinner, you would like to read a charming story about Harry's Bar, find a collection of Ernest Hemingway's short stories that includes his amusing and provocative "The Good Lion."

My assistant Amanda O'Brien collects unusual china—and these square plates decorated with huge, mauve-pink roses are the ultimate. We set them on my green and white enamel-top kitchen table, like flowers on a trellis, and topped them with carpaccio and with a very interesting pasta and pumpkin dish.

MENU

CARPACCIO WITH RED LETTUCE
FETTUCCINE WITH PUMPKIN-CREAM SAUCE
COFFEE SHERBET

Carpaccio with Red Lettuce

SERVES 4

Mustard-Garlic Mayonnaise
- 1 egg, at room temperature
  Juice of ½ lemon
- ⅜ teaspoon salt
  Pinch of cayenne pepper
- 1 clove garlic, peeled and finely minced
- 1 teaspoon Dijon mustard
- 7 tablespoons vegetable oil
- 3 tablespoons light olive oil

- ½ pound piece Parmesan cheese
- ½ pound lean filet of beef, all fat removed and meat sliced paper thin
- 1 small head red leaf lettuce, washed and dried

1. To make the mayonnaise, blend all ingredients except the oils at high speed in a blender jar until thoroughly mixed. With the motor still running, add the oils, a few drops at a time, until the mixture begins to thicken; pour in the remaining oil in a steady stream until well combined. Refrigerate.

2. Use a sharp cheese slicer to make thin curls of cheese by pulling it across the top surface of the Parmesan cheese.

3. Divide and arrange the lettuce leaves on 4 individual plates. Place several slices of raw beef on the greens and drizzle with the mayonnaise. Top with slices of Parmesan cheese and serve immediately.

Fettuccine with Pumpkin-Cream Sauce

SERVES 4

1 small (approximately 1¼ pounds) sugar pumpkin, peeled and seeded
1 shallot, peeled and finely minced
2½ tablespoons unsalted butter
Pinch of ground mace
1 cup heavy cream
2 egg yolks, lightly beaten
Salt and freshly ground black pepper
½ bulb fresh fennel, trimmed and julienned into 2½-inch strips
1 pound fettuccine, preferably fresh
⅓ pound prosciutto, trimmed and finely julienned
Freshly grated Parmesan cheese

1. Julienne enough of the pumpkin flesh into 2½-inch-long strips to yield 1 cup. Set aside. Cut the remaining pumpkin meat into 1-inch cubes and steam them over boiling water until very, very tender, approximately 15 to 25 minutes.

2. In a small saucepan, sauté the shallot in ½ tablespoon butter until soft but not browned, 3 to 5 minutes. Puree the sautéed shallot in a food processor with the steamed pumpkin and mace until completely smooth.

3. In a small, heavy saucepan, reduce the cream by one-half. Remove from the heat and, stirring continuously, whisk in the egg yolks, a bit at a time, until well blended. Beat in 1¼ to 1½ cups of the pumpkin puree and season to taste. Return the saucepan to low heat and heat the cream sauce through; do not cook it any further.

4. In a medium skillet, melt the remaining butter and sauté the fennel and pumpkin strips over medium-low heat until softened, 7 to 10 minutes; do not brown. Add the prosciutto and heat through. Set aside and keep warm.

5. Cook the fettuccine in a large pot of boiling water until tender. Drain well.

6. Toss the fettuccine with the cream sauce. Serve immediately with the vegetable-prosciutto mixture and the Parmesan cheese.

Coffee Sherbet

MAKES 1 PINT

4 cups freshly brewed hot, strong coffee
⅔ cup sugar
½ cup milk
Amaretto biscuits

1. Combine the hot coffee and sugar in a medium bowl and stir until sugar is completely dissolved.

2. Add the milk to the coffee and chill thoroughly.

3. Freeze the coffee mixture in an ice-cream maker according to the manufacturer's directions.

4. Serve a scoop of the coffee sherbet in a dessert dish with amaretto biscuits.

Roast Pork with Onions and Prunes

Often on a winter Sunday, Mother would set a roast loin of pork on the table, with mashed potatoes, pureed, steamed, or sautéed green vegetables, and maybe a salad or two; a hearty soup and several desserts began and ended the meal. We were three active boys and three hungry girls, and after church, Sunday school, and a long walk home, we were ready for a hearty meal.

Mother had her tricks: the loin of pork was always covered with grated yellow onion, bay leaves, salt, and pepper and was roasted, covered, until very tender. I always use a dry marinade for pork—I think it does wonders for the meat—and I like to add garlic to the roasting pan.

Mashed potatoes were made in great quantity—Mother always added cream cheese, milk or cream, and lots of freshly ground black pepper. Butternut squash, pumpkin, carrots, turnips, peas, and even broccoli were pureed: the vegetables were cooked to tenderness in a pressure cooker and then put through a ricer or a food mill. If Mother thought the vegetables were not tasty enough, she added an apple or an onion while they were cooking and pureed them together.

The fresh pineapple sorbet tastes perfect after such a warm, comforting meal. You can make similar ices using apricot or papaya nectars or grapefruit or orange juices; children love them, and they are very healthy.

For this meal of roast pork with mashed potatoes and pureed butternut squash, I chose plates from my collection of old silver luster, made in England by Johnson Bros., pearl-handled flatware by Joseph Rogers & Sons, and a bouquet of peony tulips tucked into a silver biscuit container.

M E N U

SALAD OF MÂCHE AND LIMESTONE LETTUCE
ROAST PORK WITH ONIONS AND PRUNES
PUREED BUTTERNUT SQUASH
MASHED POTATOES
PINEAPPLE SORBET

Salad of Mâche and Limestone Lettuce

SERVES 4

1 handful of a combination of mâche and limestone lettuce per person

Vinaigrette
MAKES ½ CUP
3 tablespoons blueberry or raspberry vinegar
⅓ cup olive oil

1 teaspoon Dijon mustard
Salt and freshly ground black pepper

Combine the greens in a large serving bowl. Whisk together all the vinaigrette ingredients until well blended; season to taste. Toss with the salad greens and serve.

Roast Pork
with Onions and Prunes

SERVES 4

1 (3½-pound) loin of pork, bone in, notched between the chops
2 teaspoons coarse salt
1 teaspoon freshly ground black pepper
5 or 6 bay leaves, preferably fresh
½ cup pitted prunes
½ cup Armagnac
3 onions, peeled and root ends cut off
6 to 8 cloves garlic, peeled
½ cup dry white wine
5 tablespoons unsalted butter
12 shallots, peeled and left whole
½ pound assorted small wild mushrooms (I use a combination of shiitakes, chanterelles, and brown field mushrooms), quartered
¼ cup chopped fresh flat Italian parsley

1. Rub the pork with the salt and pepper and place the bay leaves on top. Let rest at room temperature for at least 30 minutes.

2. Macerate the prunes in ⅓ cup Armagnac for at least 30 minutes.

3. Preheat the oven to 425° F. Line a roasting pan with aluminum foil.

4. Place the meat in the foil-lined pan. Coarsely grate the onions over the pork, saving the pointed tops of each. Arrange the onion tops and garlic on the pork. Roast for 20 minutes.

5. Remove the pork from the oven and loosely cover it with aluminum foil. Return it to the oven and cook until a meat thermometer registers 170° F., approximately 50 minutes longer.

6. Remove the pork from the pan and add the remaining Armagnac and the white wine to the roasting pan. Scrape up any bits of cooked pork and other drippings and pour the entire mixture into a small saucepan. Reduce by one-half over high heat.

7. In a small skillet, melt 2 tablespoons butter and sauté the shallots until golden brown, about 5 minutes. Add the macerated prunes with their liquid and the reduced pan drippings. Sauté over medium-low heat until thoroughly warmed, a few minutes.

8. In a large skillet, melt the remaining 3 tablespoons butter and sauté the mushrooms for 4 minutes. Stir in the parsley.

9. Cut the pork into individual chops and serve with the mushrooms and some of the shallot and prune sauce. (Reserve some of the sauce for the mashed potatoes.)

Pureed Butternut Squash

SERVES 4

1 small butternut squash (about 1 pound), peeled, seeded, and cut into small pieces
4 tablespoons (½ stick) unsalted butter
¼ cup heavy cream
¼ teaspoon ground ginger
Salt and freshly ground black pepper

1. Steam the squash over boiling water until tender, 20 to 25 minutes. Remove to the bowl of a food processor and puree until smooth.

2. Add the butter, cream, and ginger to the food processor and puree until smooth. Season to taste and serve hot.

NOTE: The puree can be prepared ahead of time and reheated in the top of a double boiler.

Mashed Potatoes

SERVES 4

4 boiling potatoes, peeled and cut into
   pieces
½ cup (1 stick) unsalted butter, at room
   temperature
3 ounces cream cheese, at room
   temperature
⅓ cup Crème Fraîche (page 11)
   Salt and freshly ground white pepper

1. Cook the potatoes in a large pot of boiling water until tender, about 20 to 25 minutes. Drain well and beat in the bowl of an electric mixer, adding the butter bit by bit.

2. Add the cream cheese and crème fraîche, beating until smooth. Season well.

3. Keep potatoes hot in the top of a double boiler until ready to serve with the remaining shallot and prune sauce spooned on top.

NOTE: Do not use a food processor to make these potatoes or they will be gluey.

Pineapple Sorbet

MAKES APPROXIMATELY 1 PINT

2 cups unsweetened pineapple juice
1 tablespoon coconut cream
   Juice and zest of 1 lime

2 ripe kiwifruits

Combine the ingredients. Place the mixture in an ice-cream maker and freeze according to the manufacturer's directions. Serve garnished with slices of ripe kiwifruit.

The pineapple sorbet with kiwifruit is served on a beautiful Limoges plate rimmed in luster, from a set that Andy's mother gave us. The napkins and tablecloth are green mottled damask.

Skillet Chicken with Watercress

I am a firm believer in serving all types of food to all types of people. Not every meal for guests has to be gourmet: often, guests want the simpler things, and that is what this menu is all about.

The skillet chicken was inspired by a dish I was served in North Carolina. I think that my hostess used squab, but fresh poussins or young chickens—not Cornish hens—work beautifully. Presented on a bed of watercress or very young spinach leaves, this entrée can be served at a country lunch or a more formal dinner party.

My good friend Zacki Murphy from North Carolina was in Connecticut the day we photographed this menu, and she made this delectable spoonbread, or cornmeal soufflé. My sister Laura Herbert created the black-eyed pea salad. She found that a good variety of canned peas works well, unless you are lucky enough to find fresh peas.

The raspberry cobbler can be made at any time of the year because fresh or frozen berries can be used. I grow all types of berries and always have more than I can use in season. Spread out on cookie sheets, they will freeze in a couple of hours and can be packed loosely in airtight containers. Then they can be used whole or turned into purees, syrups, or jellies throughout the year.

M E N U

SKILLET CHICKEN WITH WATERCRESS
SPOONBREAD
BLACK-EYED PEA SALAD
RASPBERRY COBBLER

Skillet Chicken with Watercress

SERVES 4

4 *tiny (¾ to 1 pound) poussins, or 2 small chickens (about 2½ pounds each)*
¾ *cup (1½ sticks) unsalted butter*
2 *bunches watercress, washed and stemmed*
  Salt and freshly ground black pepper

1. Using a very sharp knife, remove the backbone, breastbone, and cartilage from each chicken. Cut chickens in half and remove ribs carefully, keeping breast halves intact.

2. In a large skillet, melt the butter over medium heat and add the chickens, skin side down. Cook, uncovered, until the chicken is golden, about 15 minutes; turn over and continue cooking, uncovered, for 20 to 25 minutes.

3. Place the watercress on a platter and top with the chickens; the heat from the chicken will steam the watercress. Season to taste and serve immediately.

Spoonbread

SERVES 4

⅔ *cup yellow or white cornmeal*
1 *teaspoon salt*
1 *tablespoon sugar*
2 *cups milk, scalded*
2 *tablespoons (¼ stick) unsalted butter, at room temperature*
3 *eggs, separated*
2 *teaspoons baking powder*
  Pinch of salt

1. Preheat the oven to 350° F. Lightly butter a 1-quart charlotte mold or soufflé dish.

2. Combine the cornmeal, salt, and sugar and stir slowly into the scalded milk. Over low heat, blend in the butter. Remove the saucepan from the heat and beat in the egg yolks and baking powder. Let cool.

3. Beat the egg whites with a pinch of salt until stiff. Gently fold into the cornmeal mixture. Pour the batter into the prepared mold and bake until puffed and golden, 30 to 35 minutes. Serve immediately.

Black-eyed Pea Salad

SERVES 4

2 *(15-ounce) cans black-eyed peas, rinsed and drained*
2 *scallions, cut into ½-inch pieces*
1 *red bell pepper, seeded and finely chopped*
½ *green bell pepper, seeded and finely chopped (optional)*
¼ *cup chopped fresh flat Italian parsley*
¼ *cup finely chopped fresh chervil (optional)*
1 *clove garlic, peeled and finely minced*

Dressing
½ *cup olive oil*
3 *tablespoons red wine vinegar*
1 *to 2 tablespoons whole-grain mustard*
1 *fresh jalapeño, seeded and very finely minced*
  Salt and freshly ground black pepper

1. In a large salad bowl, combine peas, scallions, red and green peppers, parsley, chervil, and garlic.

2. In a small bowl, whisk together the dressing ingredients. Pour over the salad mixture, toss, and serve immediately.

Raspberry Cobbler

SERVES 4

Biscuit Topping
- 1 cup all-purpose flour
- ½ tablespoon sugar
- ⅛ teaspoon salt
- ½ cup (1 stick) unsalted butter, chilled and cut into small pieces
- 1½ tablespoons ice water
- 2 tablespoons heavy cream

- 2 (10-ounce) packages unsweetened frozen whole raspberries
- ¼ cup sugar

Whipped cream (optional)

1. Preheat the oven to 425° F.

2. Combine the flour, sugar, and salt in a medium bowl. Cut in the butter until the mixture resembles coarse meal. A few drops at a time, add just enough ice water to hold the dough together. Place the pastry on a lightly floured board and roll into a rectangle with a thickness of ⅛ inch. Chill 20 minutes.

3. Place the raspberries in the bottom of a shallow baking dish measuring approximately 5 × 10 inches. Sprinkle evenly with 3 tablespoons sugar.

4. Place the biscuit topping over the raspberries and crimp the edges. Cut a decorative pattern in the top, brush with the cream, and sprinkle with the remaining tablespoon of sugar. Bake until the pastry is golden brown and the fruit juices are bubbling in the center, about 25 minutes. Serve warm with whipped cream, if desired.

Everyone loves fruit cobblers, and this one, made with raspberries, is especially delicious; I baked it in a Pillivuyt ovenproof dish and served it on amethyst plates with generous dollops of softly whipped cream.

Marinated Veal Chops

The veal chops, acorn squash rings, and lima beans are served on Wedgewood plates; the radicchio and watercress salad is on Kingsware; the wine goblets are my treasured amethyst Depression glass; and the cloth is taupe cotton lace.

Chops, like any cut of veal, can be easily overcooked. I find that marinating them in a flavorful Merlot, baking them under parchment to contain their moisture, and then quickly broiling them to enhance their appearance preserves the delicacy of this tender, young meat.

Acorn squashes are now grown both with the traditional dark green skin and in a bright orange. The flesh of the latter is perhaps a bit brighter in color, but I have really had no luck in determining any difference in flavor—I enjoy both of them. I always find that half a squash is too much for one serving, so I devised this way of cooking them. The crosswise slices are very attractive, and the flesh cooks much more quickly when sliced. The brown sugar and butter glaze the squash and make it especially tasty.

In our garden we grow lima beans every year, and every fall we harvest about four or five dinners' worth. With such a small crop—limas are not prolific producers—I do not freeze our own beans but use store-bought baby limas, a quick acceptable substitute, out of season.

I make these caramel oranges often, and everyone loves them. The fresh caramel sauce, by the way, can also be used over ice cream—it's especially good over lemon ice cream or red currant ice cream.

MENU

RADICCHIO AND WATERCRESS SALAD
MARINATED VEAL CHOPS
SAUTÉED LIMA BEANS
BAKED ACORN SQUASH RINGS
CARAMEL ORANGES

Radicchio and Watercress Salad

SERVES 2

1 *bunch watercress*
½ *head radicchio, cut into small wedges*

Lemon-Honey Dressing
MAKES APPROXIMATELY ¼ CUP
Juice of 1 lemon
1 *tablespoon honey*
1 *tablespoon safflower oil*
Salt and freshly ground black pepper

Combine the watercress and radicchio wedges in a serving bowl. In a small bowl, whisk together the dressing ingredients. Toss with the radicchio and watercress right before serving.

A good, thick veal chop weighs 1 to 1½ pounds—really too much for one serving, but that's what makes veal chops so luxurious.

Below right: *The acorn squash rings were baked in another of my tin-lined copper pans.*

Marinated Veal Chops

SERVES 2

2   *loin veal chops, 1½ inches thick*
2   *tablespoons olive oil*
½   *cup dry red wine, preferably Merlot*
    Juice of 1 lemon
    Salt and freshly ground black pepper
2   *large shallots, peeled and sliced*
2   *cloves garlic, peeled and sliced*
2   *tablespoons (¼ stick) unsalted butter, melted*

1. Preheat the oven to 450° F. Place the veal chops in a baking dish.

2. In a small bowl, combine the oil, wine, and lemon juice. Pour the mixture over the veal chops, sprinkle with salt and pepper, and arrange the shallot and garlic slices on top of the chops. Marinate at room temperature for 30 minutes or overnight in the refrigerator.

3. Drizzle the butter over the tops of the veal chops and cover loosely with parchment paper. Bake 30 minutes or until done to your liking.

4. Remove the chops from the oven and discard the parchment paper. Place under a preheated broiler just until the tops are browned. Serve immediately.

Sautéed Lima Beans

SERVES 2

1   *(10-ounce) package frozen baby lima beans*
2   *tablespoons (¼ stick) unsalted butter*
    Salt and freshly ground black pepper

Thaw the lima beans. In a medium skillet, .melt the butter over medium heat. Sauté the lima beans until heated through, 4 to 5 minutes. Season to taste and serve hot.

Baked Acorn Squash Rings

SERVES 2

1   *small acorn squash*
4   *tablespoons (½ stick) unsalted butter, cut into pieces*
    Salt and freshly ground black pepper
⅓   *cup dark brown sugar, tightly packed*

1. Preheat the oven to 350° F.

2. Cut the unpeeled squash crosswise into ½-inch slices and place them on a cutting board. Using a biscuit cutter slightly larger than the seed center, cut out the seeds from each ring and discard.

3. Place the squash rings on a lightly buttered baking sheet. Dot each ring with butter and season to taste. Sprinkle a bit of brown sugar over each ring.

4. Bake the squash for 15 minutes. Turn the rings over, dot with more butter and sugar, and bake until tender, 5 to 10 minutes longer. Serve hot.

Caramel Oranges

SERVES 2

Caramel Syrup
 ½ cup sugar
 2 tablespoons water
 ½ cup heavy cream

 2 oranges, carefully peeled

1. In a heavy, medium saucepan, combine the sugar and water over medium heat and cook until the sugar dissolves. Do not stir or the mixture may become cloudy; swirl the pan occasionally to mix the ingredients. Continue to cook over medium heat until the sugar begins to caramelize and the syrup turns brown in color.

2. Remove pan from the heat and quickly whisk in the cream. (If necessary, return the pan to the heat to completely incorporate the cream.) Off the heat, as the syrup sets and cools, it will thicken.

3. Cut off the top and bottom ends of each orange. Standing the oranges upright on a cutting surface, trim away all the peel, white pith, and membrane with a very sharp knife.

4. To serve, place each orange on an individual dessert plate and spoon some warm caramel syrup around the fruit.

The fanciful bird pattern painted on this Kingsware plate is left exposed by the caramel orange dessert.

Herb-Garden Leg of Lamb

Almost everyone I know loves a good roast leg of lamb, and over the years I have learned all sorts of ways to present this dish. Sometimes I glaze the lamb with guava jelly and garlic; sometimes I coat it with herbed mustard and bread crumbs; I may butterfly and grill it after marinating it for a bit in olive oil and lemon juice; or perhaps I roast it, as I did in this recipe, with lots of garlic, rosemary, sage, and olive oil.

My English friend Julia Booth-Clibborn always cooks her scalloped potatoes this way, in true Quick Cook fashion. By precooking the slices of potato in cream before arranging them in the casserole, the baking time is reduced from an hour to about twenty minutes. To continue this winter meal, cook up some yellow turnip and butternut squash with herbs for flavor: I use rosemary, but thyme or winter savory would also be good. The salad makes use of winter greens; the Gorgonzola cheese and toasted walnuts are my special additions.

I love baked fruits, and these spiced pears are fancy looking without being complicated to make. I bake the pears in porcelain baking dishes: they are pretty and look good on most dessert plates.

These wonderful old plates with their pine cone and needle design were made for a Lake Tahoe diner called The Pine Tree, or so I've been told. Whatever the truth of the story, the plates make a perfect background for a winter dinner of lamb with rosemary-scented vegetables and scalloped potatoes.

M E N U
WINTER SALAD WITH TOASTED WALNUTS AND CHEESE
HERB-GARDEN LEG OF LAMB
POTATOES SCALLOPED IN CREAM
VEGETABLES WITH ROSEMARY
BAKED SPICED PEARS

Winter Salad with Toasted Walnuts and Cheese

SERVES 6

Dressing
½ cup vegetable oil, preferably
   safflower
⅓ cup white wine vinegar
¼ cup walnut oil
1 tablespoon Dijon mustard
   Salt and freshly ground black pepper

1 handful of a combination of
   escarole and curly chicory per person
½ cup toasted walnut halves (see Note)
½ cup crumbled blue cheese (we used
   Mountain Blue Gorgonzola)

1. Combine the vegetable oil, vinegar, walnut oil, and mustard in a large bowl, whisking until thick and creamy. Season to taste.

2. Add the remaining ingredients to the bowl and toss. Serve immediately.

NOTE: To toast walnuts, place them in a preheated 350° F. oven until crisp, about 15 minutes.

Herb-Garden Leg of Lamb

SERVES 6

1 (6-pound) leg of lamb, very well trimmed
5 cloves garlic, peeled and thinly slivered
  Approximately 20 small sprigs fresh rosemary, preferably flowering
  Approximately 20 small sprigs fresh tricolor or gray sage
¼ cup green olive oil
  Salt and freshly ground black pepper

1. With the point of a small, sharp knife, make thin, deep slits all over the leg of lamb; insert the garlic slivers and herb sprigs in the slits. Drizzle the lamb with the olive oil and sprinkle with salt and pepper. Let marinate at room temperature for 20 minutes.

2. Preheat the oven to 425° F.

3. Place the lamb on a rack set in a roasting pan and cook for 1 hour. Remove the lamb from the oven and let stand for 10 minutes before carving.

I was thinking about the design for my new herb garden when I prepared this leg of lamb and found myself making little plantings all over the meat with sprigs of fresh rosemary and sage.

Potatoes Scalloped in Cream

SERVES 6

2 cups heavy cream
6 to 8 large, waxy potatoes, peeled and cut into even ⅛-inch-thick slices
1 clove garlic, peeled
  Salt and freshly ground black pepper

1. Preheat the oven to 375° F. Butter a shallow casserole and set aside.

2. In a large, heavy saucepan, heat the cream to boiling. Add the sliced potatoes and garlic and simmer until the potatoes are tender, 10 to 15 minutes.

3. Spoon the potatoes, garlic, and cream into the casserole and season to taste. Bake until the top browns slightly and the cream thickens, about 20 minutes. Serve hot.

Vegetables with Rosemary

SERVES 6

2 tablespoons olive oil
1 tablespoon unsalted butter
1 large turnip, peeled and cut into 2-inch-long strips
½ butternut squash, peeled and cut into 2-inch-long strips
2 small sprigs fresh rosemary

1. Heat the olive oil and butter in a large skillet and add the turnip pieces. Sauté over medium heat for 5 minutes; do not brown.

2. Add the squash and rosemary sprigs to the skillet and cook until all vegetables are tender, 5 to 7 minutes longer. Serve immediately.

Baked Spiced Pears

SERVES 6

3 ripe, firm Bartlett pears, peeled
6 small cinnamon sticks
6 tablespoons dark brown sugar
1½ teaspoons ground cinnamon
  Freshly grated nutmeg
6 teaspoons (¼ stick) unsalted butter
¾ cup dark rum or cognac
  Heavy cream or Crème Fraîche (page 11)

1. Preheat the oven to 350° F. Butter 6 small baking dishes (they should be just slightly larger than the pear halves), or 1 large dish.

2. Halve the pears lengthwise and remove the cores. Place them cut side

down on a board, and cut each half crosswise into 5 or 6 even slices, being careful to retain the shape of the pear. Place each half in an individual baking dish and "slide" the slices to make them fan out a bit.

3. Place 1 cinnamon stick on the side of each pear half and sprinkle each half with 1 tablespoon brown sugar, ¼ teaspoon cinnamon, and nutmeg to taste. Dot each with 1 teaspoon butter and bake until the pears are tender, 20 to 25 minutes.

4. Remove the pears from the oven and pour 2 tablespoons of the dark rum or cognac over each. Return to the oven for 5 minutes.

5. Serve the pears warm with heavy cream or crème fraîche.

These Bartlett pears, halved and arranged in individual porcelain fluted dishes with spices, butter, and rum, are simply delicious.

Monkfish with Lemon and Capers

Few things are as satisfying as making pasta. The whole process is so homey —the kneading of the dough into a smooth, soft mass, the rolling and cutting of the noodles, and the display of the finished pasta on the drying rack. I like to make lots of pasta at once, and I usually do at least a double batch of each kind. Wrapped in plastic, homemade pasta freezes very well and is an excellent thing to have on hand.

Puttanesca sauce is a spicy mixture of tomatoes, red-hot pepper flakes, garlic, and capers. I add olives and even arugula leaves. A friend has made pasta with puttanesca his special dish, and he serves it regularly, varying it according to what he has in his pantry, but always including capers, garlic, black olives, and oregano.

Monkfish fillets are strange looking—the flesh, when cooked, looks as if it has been sliced into thin strips. It cooks quickly and is extremely tender. The large imported capers can be found packed in brine or in rock salt; I prefer the latter. Well rinsed, they can be sautéed in clarified butter until crispy.

And for dessert —a chocolate fizz made from homemade hot fudge sauce, ice cream, and seltzer. For real chocoholics, serve a wedge of chocolate cake on the side.

MENU
FETTUCCINE WITH PUTTANESCA SAUCE
MONKFISH WITH LEMON AND CAPERS
CHOCOLATE FIZZ

Fettuccine with Puttanesca Sauce

SERVES 4 GENEROUSLY

Pasta
3½ cups all-purpose flour, approximately
1 teaspoon salt
5 eggs
1 tablespoon olive oil
2 tablespoons tomato paste

Puttanesca Sauce
3 tablespoons olive oil
1 clove garlic, peeled and finely minced
½ onion, peeled and chopped
¾ pound ripe plum tomatoes, seeded and chopped
1 yellow bell pepper, seeded and cut into ½-inch squares
1 red bell pepper, seeded and cut into ½-inch squares
½ cup imported oil-cured black olives, halved and pitted
8 fresh basil leaves, finely shredded
½ tablespoon fresh oregano leaves
½ teaspoon red pepper flakes
⅓ pound arugula leaves
Salt and freshly ground black pepper

Freshly grated Parmesan cheese

1. To make the pasta, combine the flour and salt on a large, flat board. Make a well in the center and break the eggs into it; add the olive oil and tomato paste. Gently incorporate these ingredients with a fork, then knead the dough with the heels of your hands until smooth, approximately 5 minutes. (If the dough is sticky, add more flour.)

2. Using a pasta machine, roll out the dough to the desired thickness. Set the machine to fettuccine width and pass the noodles through it. Store well wrapped in freezer until ready to use.

3. To make the sauce, heat the oil in a large skillet and sauté the garlic and onion until tender, 4 to 5 minutes. Add the tomatoes and cook 4 minutes longer; add the peppers and sauté until softened, 4 to 5 minutes. Stir in the olives, herbs, and red pepper flakes. Add the arugula and cook until wilted, 4 to 5 minutes. Season to taste.

4. Cook the pasta in a large pot of boiling water just until tender, 2 to 4 minutes. Drain well.

5. Serve the pasta with the hot sauce and the Parmesan cheese.

Monkfish with Lemon and Capers

SERVES 4

2 lemons
1 cup (2 sticks) unsalted butter
4 (½-pound) monkfish fillets, cleaned and trimmed of veins
1 cup large imported capers, drained

1. With a sharp knife, cut strips of lemon peel ½ inch wide and 1 inch long. Set aside. (Take care to cut only the peel and none of the pith.)

2. Melt the butter in a heavy saucepan over high heat. When it begins to bubble, remove from the heat and skim off the foam. Strain the clear liquid at the top and discard any milky residue.

3. Heat half the clarified butter in a large skillet and sauté the monkfish, turning occasionally, until nearly done, about 10 minutes. Add the lemon peel and sauté until fish is browned, about 3 to 5 minutes.

4. Heat the remaining clarified butter in a small skillet until brown, about 7 minutes. Add the capers and sauté until crispy, 2 to 3 minutes.

5. Serve the monkfish fillets with the sautéed lemon peel, browned butter, and capers.

This chocolate fizz, served in a ruby goblet in front of a leaded window in the hall, is similar to an egg cream— a traditional New York drink that contains neither egg nor cream.

Chocolate Fizz

SERVES 4

2 *pints chocolate ice cream*
½ *cup Hot Fudge Sauce (page 44), at room temperature*
Seltzer water

1. Place 2 scoops of chocolate ice cream into 4 tall glasses. Pour 1 table-spoon Hot Fudge Sauce into each glass.

2. Fill the glasses with seltzer and driz-zle another tablespoon of fudge sauce over each. Serve with a slice of choco-late cake or a brownie, if desired.

Saucisson Chaud with Steamed Kale

In 1961, Andy and I went to a little New York bistro called Le Veau d'Or, where we ate a wonderful dish called *saucisson chaud*—a thick, pink sausage, very meaty, redolent of garlic and pepper, served warm. Gérard, the bistro's owner, told me it came from a local sausage maker, Ugo Buzzio. I went immediately to Ugo's delicatessen on Eighth Avenue, and I have been buying sausages there ever since. The store, called Salumeria Biellese, is now run by Ugo's son, Marc, who sells the Italian sausages that they have been making there since 1925, together with wonderful boudin, pastas, and cheeses.

Saucisson à l'ail is a semidry, cured sausage; when poached in simmering water and white wine or vermouth with a bay leaf or two, it becomes succulent and juicy. I serve it the traditional French way with a warm potato salad and pickled cornichons (French vinegar-pickled gherkins). The braised endive, which tastes slightly caramelized, and pickled dill beets are wonderful accompaniments.

The apricot-rum tart can be made as individual tartlets (two halved apricots in each) or as a nine-inch tart with sliced apricots. This tart is similar to an apple tart Normande, which has a filling of fruit and a calvados-flavored custard. In this case the custard is flavored with golden rum—Mount Gay is good.

I found my first pieces of pale green Fire King china years ago in Sag Harbor and have been collecting it ever since; here a French sausage is served with steamed kale, braised endive, potato salad, and beets on Fire King dinner plates, while Fire King egg cups serve as wine goblets.

MENU

SAUCISSON CHAUD WITH STEAMED KALE
BRAISED ENDIVE
WARM FRENCH POTATO SALAD
BEETS WITH DILL AND VINEGAR
APRICOT-RUM TART

Saucisson Chaud with Steamed Kale

SERVES 6

2 *pounds* saucisson (*large French sausage*)
½ *cup dry white wine*
12 *leaves fresh kale or small collard greens, washed and fibrous stems removed*

1. Prick the sausage in several places with the point of a sharp knife and place it in a large kettle. Add water to cover and the wine, and let simmer for 30 to 40 minutes.

2. Remove the sausage from the kettle. While still warm, peel off the casing from the sausage. Cut into ½-inch slices.

3. Layer the kale or collard greens in a steamer and cook over boiling water until they have just wilted, approximately 5 minutes.

4. Divide the steamed kale among the dinner plates and place several slices of saucisson on top. Serve immediately.

Braised Endive

SERVES 6

4 tablespoons (½ stick) unsalted butter
3 large, thick Belgian endive, halved
lengthwise
Salt and freshly ground black pepper

1. Melt the butter in a skillet large enough to hold the endive. When the butter is hot, add the endive and brown well on both sides, about 7 minutes.

2. Cut a piece of parchment paper to fit the top of the skillet (this will help keep the moisture in the pan). Cover the endive with the parchment, then add the skillet lid, lower the heat, and cook for 30 minutes. Season to taste and serve immediately.

Warm French Potato Salad

SERVES 6

Vinaigrette
¼ cup dry white wine
3 tablespoons white wine vinegar
½ to ¾ cup strong olive oil
1 tablespoon Dijon mustard

7 or 8 waxy potatoes
12 cornichons, sliced lengthwise
Salt and freshly ground black pepper

1. Combine vinaigrette ingredients, whisking well, and set aside.

2. Place the potatoes in a large pot of water and boil until just tender, 20 to 30 minutes. Do not overcook the potatoes or they will become mushy. Drain well.

3. When the potatoes are just cool enough to handle, peel with a sharp paring knife and cut into ¼-inch slices. Toss the potatoes immediately with the vinaigrette and cornichons (the potatoes

must be warm to absorb the dressing) and season to taste. Serve warm or at room temperature.

Beets with Dill and Vinegar

SERVES 6

7 small beets
⅓ cup white wine vinegar
2 tablespoons sugar
1 tablespoon chopped fresh dill

1. Preheat oven to 325°F.

2. Trim the beets, scrub well, and wrap them together in a large piece of aluminum foil. Seal well and bake until the beets are tender, about 35 minutes.

3. When the beets are cool enough to handle, peel and cut them into ¼-inch slices and arrange on a serving platter.

4. In a small saucepan, combine the vinegar and sugar over low heat. Cook just until the sugar dissolves.

5. Pour the hot vinegar-sugar mixture over the beets. Let cool before sprinkling the dill on top and serving.

Apricot-Rum Tart

SERVES 6

Custard
  1 *egg*
  ⅓ *cup granulated sugar*
  ¼ *cup all-purpose flour*
  ¾ *cup heavy cream*
  ¼ *cup golden rum*
     Several pinches of freshly grated nutmeg

 12 *ripe apricots, halved, pitted, and cut into wedges*
  6 *partially baked 4½-inch Tart Shells (page 11)*
     Vanilla sugar (see Note, page 21)
  1 *teaspoon unsalted butter, in pieces*
     Confectioners' sugar

1. Preheat oven to 375° F.

2. To make the custard, beat the egg and granulated sugar until thick and pale yellow. Add the flour, beating until smooth. Stir in the cream, rum, and nutmeg to taste.

3. Arrange the apricot wedges, cut side down, in the partially baked tart shells. Sprinkle with a bit of vanilla sugar and dot with butter. Bake for 5 minutes.

4. Remove the tarts from the oven and pour the custard mixture over and around the fruit. Bake until the custard is set and golden, 30 to 35 minutes. Remove from the oven and let cool slightly.

5. Dust the top of the tart with a bit of confectioners' sugar and place it under the broiler until it browns, a few seconds. Serve warm.

An individual apricot-rum tart is served in its baking tin with an ivory-handled fork and knife.

Chicken Wings with Vegetables and Rice

The main course of this menu is based on a dish I had many years ago in Puerto Rico. I call it "poor man's paella," and if you eliminate the saffron and the shiitake mushrooms, it is even more economical. Indeed, you can make many variations of this recipe: just remember to cook each kind of vegetable separately, to brown the chicken wings well, and to use a flavorful homemade stock. Do that, and you'll have a hearty main course that needs only a salad and dessert to make a complete and satisfying menu.

This salad is a wonderful combination of baby spinach, avocado, and grapefruit sections dressed with a walnut and walnut-oil vinaigrette. Walnut oil is a wonderful addition to your pantry, but like all nut oils, it must be kept in the refrigerator. Left too long at room temperature, it will go rancid and have to be discarded.

There are two kinds of persimmon available at many greengrocers nowadays. One, the elongated California type, must be eaten very, very ripe and soft. It does not slice well and is best served whole with a silver grapefruit spoon or cooked in puddings and cakes. The flatter, harder, less orange Japanese persimmon—the kind we used for this dessert—can be served while it is hard. I slice it crosswise and douse it with ice-cold tequila, then garnish it with mint leaves (or sometimes with ripe pomegranate seeds).

The coconut madeleines are a flavorful version of Marcel Proust's favorite childhood sweet—a tender sponge cookie made in the shape of a shell. Special French-made pans are available in several different shell shapes and sizes; it is amusing to bake several kinds of madeleine and serve them from the same platter.

MENU
CHICKEN WINGS WITH VEGETABLES AND RICE
SPINACH SALAD WITH GRAPEFRUIT AND AVOCADO
PERSIMMONS WITH TEQUILA AND MINT
COCONUT MADELEINES

Chicken Wings with Vegetables and Rice

SERVES 4

This all-in-one dish of chicken wings with vegetables and rice is cooked and served in a big copper pan.

6 scallions, white and green parts finely chopped
3 cloves garlic, peeled and sliced
1 sprig fresh rosemary
2 to 3 bay leaves, fresh or dried
¼ cup olive oil, or more if needed
2 yellow or green bell peppers, seeded and cut into 1-inch squares
2 Japanese eggplants, cut into ¼-inch slices
¼ pound shiitake mushrooms (optional)
½ pound baby okra, trimmed
12 to 16 chicken wings
1½ cups long-grain rice (I use basmati)
3 cups hot Chicken Stock (page 13) or water
1 teaspoon ground cumin
Large pinch of saffron threads
Salt and freshly ground black pepper
2 to 3 tablespoons chopped fresh flat Italian parsley

1. Preheat the oven to 400° F.

2. In a large, heavy skillet or copper casserole, sauté the scallions, garlic, rosemary, and bay leaves in the olive oil for 3 to 4 minutes. Do not brown.

3. Add the peppers, eggplants, and mushrooms and sauté over high heat for 5 to 6 minutes. Add the okra and cook 2 minutes longer. Using a slotted spoon, remove the vegetables to a plate.

4. In the same skillet or casserole, sauté the chicken wings until browned (add a bit more olive oil if necessary), 5 to 6 minutes. Add the rice and sauté 2 to 3 minutes longer.

5. Return the vegetables to the skillet or casserole, add the hot stock and spices, season to taste, and cover. Simmer (without uncovering the skillet) for 5 minutes.

6. Place the skillet or casserole in the oven for 20 to 25 minutes. At this point the liquid should have been absorbed, and the rice should have puffed. Serve immediately with a sprinkling of fresh parsley.

Spinach Salad with Grapefruit and Avocado

SERVES 4

2 large bunches young, tender spinach, well washed and dried, stems removed
1 pink grapefruit, peeled, sectioned, and all pith removed
1 ripe avocado, peeled, pitted, and sliced

Walnut Dressing
MAKES 1 CUP
½ cup walnut halves
2 tablespoons walnut oil
6 tablespoons olive oil
2 tablespoons balsamic vinegar
1 small shallot or scallion, finely minced
Salt and freshly ground black pepper
Pinch of sugar

1. Arrange the spinach leaves in a large, flat bowl. Place the grapefruit and avocado pieces in a decorative pattern over the leaves.

2. In a small skillet, sauté the walnuts in walnut oil until just colored; do not brown too much. Drain and add to the other dressing ingredients, mixing well.

3. Pour the dressing over the salad, toss well, and serve immediately.

Persimmons with Tequila and Mint

SERVES 4

2 ripe, firm persimmons
Tequila
Whole mint leaves

Cut the persimmons lengthwise into ¼-inch slices. Divide the fruit among four dessert plates and top each with a splash of tequila. Garnish with fresh mint leaves and serve with Coconut Madeleines (recipe follows).

Coconut Madeleines

MAKES 36

4 eggs, at room temperature
¼ teaspoon salt
⅔ cup granulated sugar
1 teaspoon vanilla extract
1 cup all-purpose flour
½ cup (1 stick) unsalted butter, melted and cooled
⅓ cup shredded coconut
Sifted confectioners' sugar (optional)

1. Preheat the oven to 375° F. Butter and flour madeleine tins carefully.

2. Beat eggs, salt, and sugar together in the bowl of an electric mixer until very thick and fluffy, about 8 minutes. Add the vanilla. Gently but rapidly fold in the flour, then the melted butter, and finally the coconut.

3. Spoon the mixture quickly into the prepared tins and bake until golden brown, 8 to 10 minutes. Remove madeleines from tins immediately and cook on racks.

4. Sprinkle liberally with confectioners' sugar if desired and serve with the persimmons.

Madeleines have such literary glory —they play a memorable role in Marcel Proust's Remembrance of Things Past—that we sometimes forget they are just shell-shaped sponge cookies. They do look pretty, though, especially combined with slices of persimmon and garnished with a few mint leaves.

INDEX